Did you know that the capitol building in Frankfort is Kentucky's fourth capitol building? The current capitol buildi[...] [...]d in 1910.

Kentucky

HARCOURT
SOCiAL Studies

Kentucky

Harcourt
SCHOOL PUBLISHERS

www.harcourtschool.com

HARCOURT

SOCIAL Studies

Kentucky

Series Authors

Dr. Michael J. Berson
Professor
Social Science Education
University of South Florida
Tampa, Florida

Dr. Tyrone C. Howard
Associate Professor
UCLA Graduate School of Education &
    Information Studies
University of California at Los Angeles
Los Angeles, California

Dr. Cinthia Salinas
Assistant Professor
Department of Curriculum and
    Instruction
College of Education
The University of Texas at Austin
Austin, Texas

Series Consultants

Dr. Marsha Alibrandi
Assistant Professor of Social Studies
Curriculum and Instruction
    Department
North Carolina State University
Raleigh, North Carolina

Dr. Patricia G. Avery
Professor
College of Education and Human
    Development
University of Minnesota
Minneapolis/St. Paul, Minnesota

Dr. Linda Bennett
Associate Professor
College of Education
University of Missouri–Columbia
Columbia, Missouri

Dr. Walter C. Fleming
Department Head and Professor
Native American Studies
Montana State University
Bozeman, Montana

Dr. S. G. Grant
Associate Professor
University at Buffalo
Buffalo, New York

C. C. Herbison
Lecturer
African and African-American Studies
University of Kansas
Lawrence, Kansas

Dr. Eric Johnson
Assistant Professor
Director, Urban Education Program
School of Education
Drake University
Des Moines, Iowa

Dr. Bruce E. Larson
Professor
Social Studies Education
Secondary Education
Woodring College of Education
Western Washington University
Bellingham, Washington

Dr. Merry M. Merryfield
Professor
Social Studies and Global Education
College of Education
The Ohio State University
Columbus, Ohio

Dr. Peter Rees
Associate Professor
Department of Geography
University of Delaware
Wilmington, Delaware

Dr. Phillip J. VanFossen
James F. Ackerman Professor of
    Social Studies Education
Associate Director, Purdue Center for
    Economic Education
Purdue University
West Lafayette, Indiana

Dr. Myra Zarnowski
Professor
Elementary and Early Childhood
    Education
Queens College
The City University of New York
Flushing, New York

Kentucky Consultants

Dr. Carol Crowe Carraco
Professor
Department of History
Western Kentucky University
Bowling Green, Kentucky

Dr. John Kleber
Commonwealth Fellow
McConnell Center for
    Political Leadership
University of Louisville
Louisville, Kentucky

Dr. Richard Ulack
Professor
Department of Geography
University of Kentucky
Lexington, Kentucky

Dr. Fay A. Yarbrough
Assistant Professor
Department of History
University of Kentucky
Lexington, Kentucky

Classroom Reviewers and Contributors

Craig Carter
Teacher
Graves County Central Elementary
    School
Mayfield, Kentucky

Regina Dawson
Teacher
Clays Mill Elementary School
Lexington, Kentucky

Shena Rose
Teacher
Oak Grove Elementary School
Corbin, Kentucky

Lee Ann White
Teacher
Morgantown Elementary School
Morgantown, Kentucky

SCHOOL PUBLISHERS

Maps
researched and prepared by

ISBN-13: 978-0-15-349859-6
ISBN-10: 0-15-349859-5

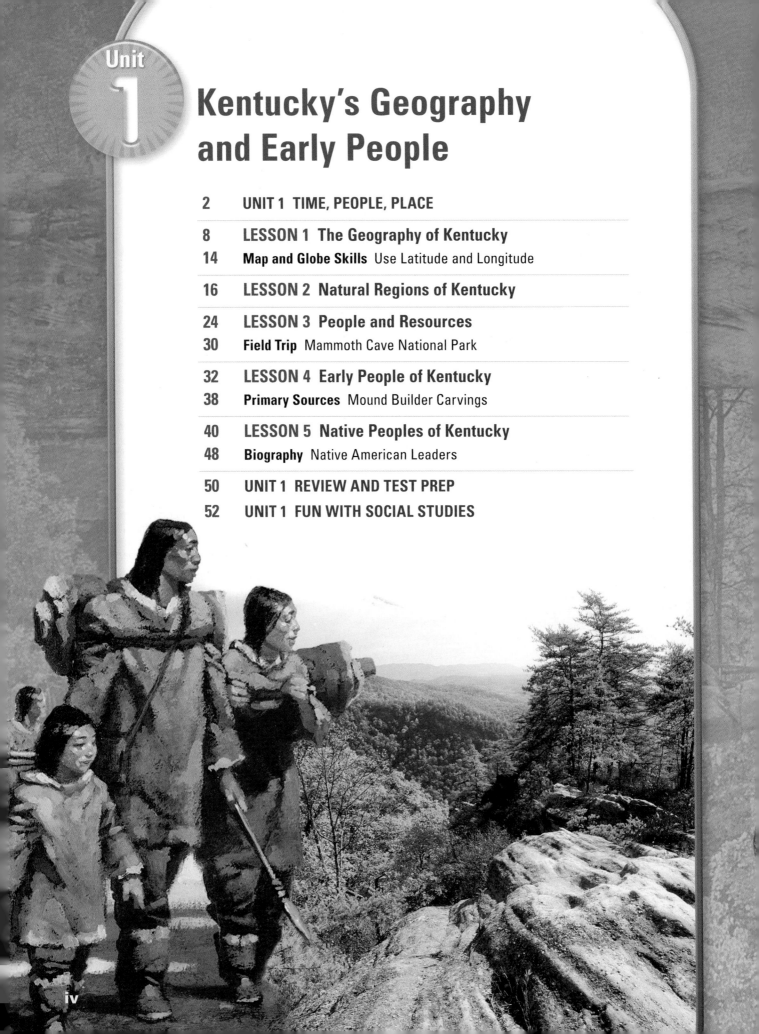

Unit 1

Kentucky's Geography and Early People

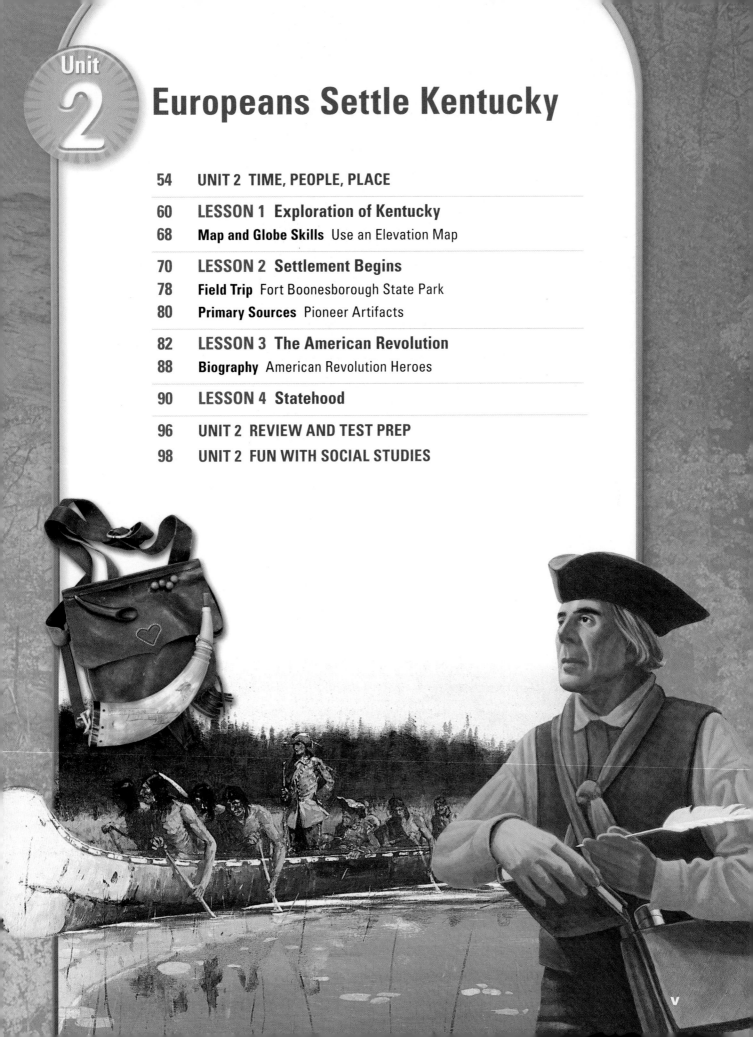

Unit 2 Europeans Settle Kentucky

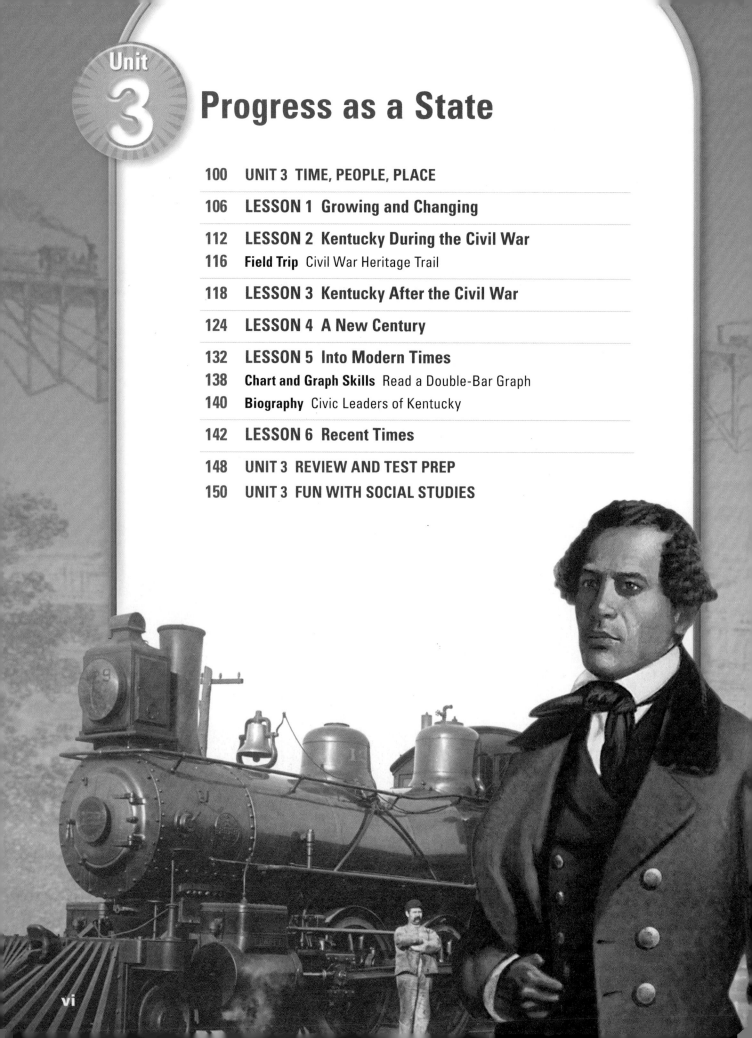

Unit 3

Progress as a State

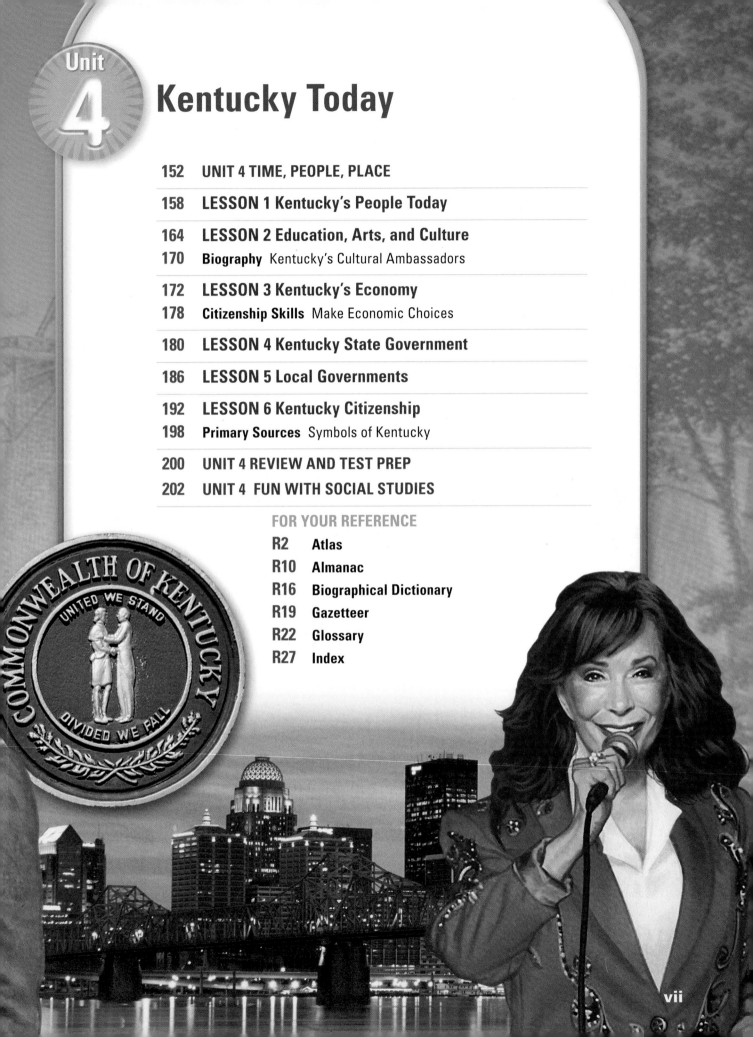

Unit 4

Kentucky Today

Features

Kentucky's Geography and Early People

 Start with the Standards

Kentucky Core Content for Assessment

SS-04-3.1.1 Students will describe scarcity and explain how scarcity requires people in Kentucky to make economic choices and incur opportunity costs.

SS-04-3.4.1 Students will describe production, distribution and consumption of goods and services in regions of Kentucky and the U.S.

SS-04-4.1.1 Students will use geographic tools to identify and describe natural resources and other physical characteristics in regions of Kentucky and the United States.

SS-04-4.1.2 Students will use geographic tools to locate major landforms, bodies of water, places and objects in Kentucky by their absolute and relative locations.

SS-04-4.1.3 Students will describe how different factors influence where human activities were/are located in Kentucky.

SS-04-4.2.1 Students will compare regions in Kentucky and the United States by their human characteristics and physical characteristics.

SS-04-4.3.1 Students will describe patterns of human settlement in regions of Kentucky and explain how these patterns were/are influenced by physical characteristics.

SS-04-4.3.2 Students will describe how advances in technology allow people to settle in places previously inaccessible in Kentucky.

The Big Idea

Geography
People in Kentucky have always interacted with their environment and been affected by it.

What to Know

- Where in the world is Kentucky located?
- How are each of Kentucky's natural regions different?
- How do people use Kentucky's natural resources?
- Which people lived in Kentucky first and how did Kentucky's environment shape their way of life?
- Who were the Native Americans that lived in Kentucky, and how did they interact with their environment?

Time

Kentucky's Geography and Early People

About 12,500 years ago
People arrive in what is now Kentucky, p. 33

About 10,000 years ago
Archaic Indians begin to barter for materials to make tools, p. 34

15,000 years ago

10,000 years ago

At the Same Time

 About **10,000** years ago
People in southwestern Asia begin to grow crops and raise animals

 About **6,200** years ago
The Egyptians develop a calendar

Kentucky's Geography and Early People

About **3,000** years ago
Native Kentuckians start growing corn and beans, p. 35

About **1,000** years ago
Mississippians build mounds in what is now Kentucky, p. 36

5,000 years ago

Present

About **5,500** years ago
The earliest cities form in southwestern Asia

About **4,000** years ago
Native Americans begin to settle in villages in what is now the western United States

About **1,600** years ago
Christianity becomes the official religion of the Roman Empire

Paleo-Indians

Adena

People

Paleo-Indians

- About 12,000 years ago, were the first people to reach Kentucky
- Probably came to North America from Asia by crossing a land bridge
- Hunted animals and gathered wild plants for food

Adena

- Appeared about 3,000 years ago
- Lived mainly in villages along the Ohio River
- Built huge mounds as burial places and centers of worship
- Made clay pottery

Shawnee

- Lived in villages along the Ohio River and in central Kentucky
- Relied mainly on farming to survive but also hunted and fished
- Had as many as 100 homes in some villages

Shawnee

Cherokee

Chickasaw

- Lived in the Mississippi Embayment Region
- Were known as fierce warriors

Cherokee

- Many lived in the valleys of southeastern Kentucky
- Families lived together and were called according to the mother's family name
- Cherokee men mainly hunted and the women grew crops

Iroquois

- Were a group of different tribes who united to avoid conflicts
- Lived mainly in New York but eventually spread out into Kentucky
- Lived in longhouses

Chickasaw

Iroquois

ILLINOIS

Western Kentucky Coal Field Region

The Knobs Region

Ohio River

Mississippi River

Green River

Rough River

Rough River Lake

Nolin River Lake

WESTERN KENTUCKY COAL FIELD

Barren River Lake

Barren River

Tennessee River

Lake Barkley

▼ Mississippi River 257 ft.

MISSISSIPPI EMBAYMENT (JACKSON PURCHASE)

The Breaks

Dripping Springs Escarpment

Kentucky Lake

```
0        25        50 Miles
0    25     50 Kilometers
Albers Equal-Area Projection
```

△ Highest point

▼ Lowest point

▲ Mountain peak

— Natural region border

— Subregion border

— State border

Mississippi Embayment Region

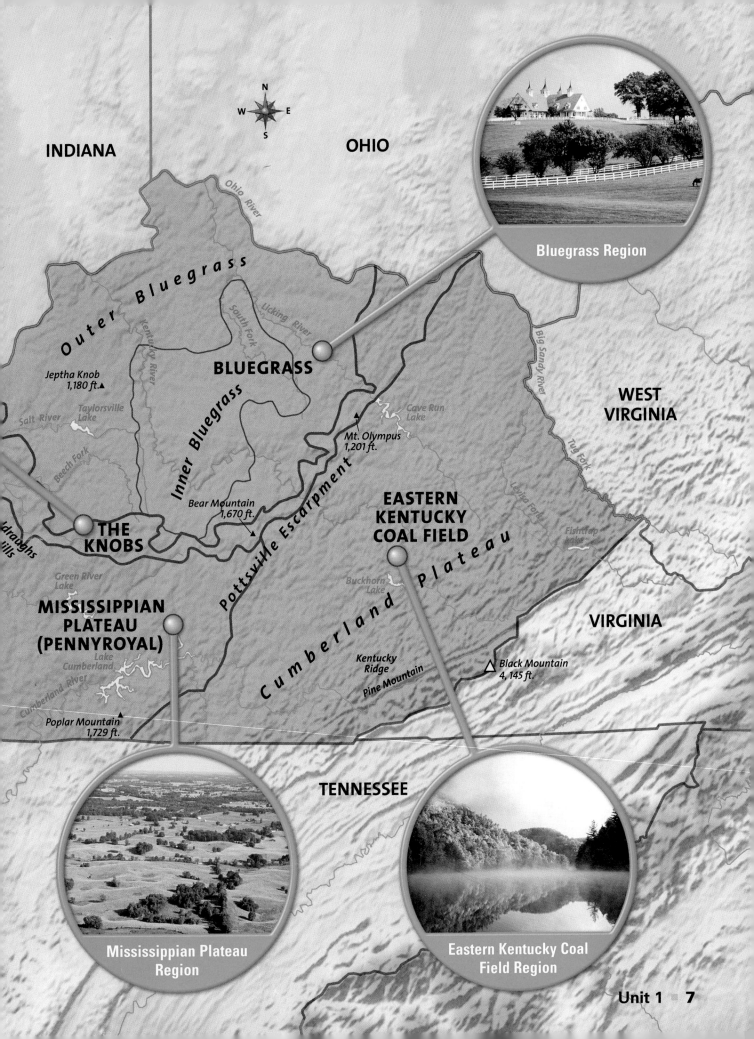

INDIANA

OHIO

N
W · E
S

Ohio River

Bluegrass Region

Outer Bluegrass

Licking River

South Fork

Kentucky River

Jeptha Knob
1,180 ft.▲

BLUEGRASS

Inner Bluegrass

Taylorsville
Lake

Salt River

Beech Fork

Mt. Olympus
1,201 ft.

Cave Run
Lake

Big Sandy River

WEST
VIRGINIA

Tug Fork

Bear Mountain
1,670 ft.

Pottsville Escarpment

THE
KNOBS

draughs
ills

EASTERN
KENTUCKY
COAL FIELD

Levisa Fork

Fishtrap
lake

Green River
Lake

Buckhorn
Lake

Cumberland Plateau

VIRGINIA

MISSISSIPPIAN
PLATEAU
(PENNYROYAL)

Lake
Cumberland

Cumberland River

Kentucky
Ridge
Pine Mountain

Black Mountain
4, 145 ft.

Poplar Mountain
1,729 ft.

TENNESSEE

Mississippian Plateau
Region

Eastern Kentucky Coal
Field Region

Lesson 1

The Geography of Kentucky

WHAT TO KNOW
Where is Kentucky, and what is important about its location?

VOCABULARY

hemisphere p. 9

equator p. 9

continent p. 9

relative location p. 10

region p. 10

physical characteristic p. 11

human characteristic p. 12

PLACES
Kentucky
North America
United States
Southeast
Inland South
Appalachia

MAIN IDEA AND DETAILS

Main Idea

Details

YOU ARE THERE

"You have e-mail!" your computer tells you. The message is from your new pen pal in France. Like you, she's in the fourth grade. You sent your first e-mail to her yesterday. In it, you wrote that you live in **Kentucky**. Now your pen pal is asking a lot of questions about Kentucky. She wants to know where it is, what it looks like, and what it's like to live there. Do you know enough about Kentucky's geography to answer all her questions?

CANADA

NORTH AMERICA

ATLANTIC OCEAN

MEXICO

PACIFIC OCEAN

SOUTH AMERICA

Where Is Kentucky?

Your pen pal's first question is "Where is Kentucky?" To answer, you could start by describing Kentucky's global address, or where Kentucky is on Earth.

A Global Address

First, you might tell your pen pal in which **hemisphere**, or half of Earth, Kentucky is located. An imaginary line called the **equator** divides Earth into the Northern Hemisphere and the Southern Hemisphere. Because Kentucky lies north of the equator, you write to your pen pal that Kentucky is in the Northern Hemisphere.

Another imaginary line divides Earth into the Western Hemisphere and the Eastern Hemisphere. Kentucky is west of this line, so you also write that it is in the Western Hemisphere.

To be more specific, you write, "Kentucky is on the continent of **North America**." A **continent** is one of the seven largest land areas on Earth. You then write that Kentucky is in the **United States**, the second-largest country in North America. Finally, you explain that Kentucky is one of the 50 states that make up the United States of America.

READING CHECK **◎ MAIN IDEA AND DETAILS**
In which hemispheres is Kentucky located?

Kentucky's Location

DIAGRAM On which continent is Kentucky located?

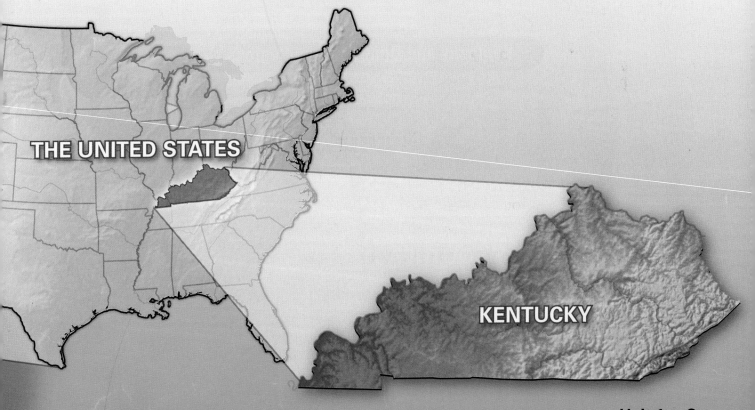

THE UNITED STATES

KENTUCKY

Relative Location

Another way to describe where you live is to give Kentucky's relative location. The **relative location** of a place is where it is in relation to other places on Earth.

Kentucky's Neighbors

You can use other states to describe Kentucky's relative location. Seven other states border Kentucky. Kentucky is located east of Missouri and north of Tennessee. It is south of Illinois, Indiana, and Ohio and west of Virginia and West Virginia.

Kentucky's location is important to its economy. Many businesses move to Kentucky because it is located within a day's drive of more than two-thirds of the people of the United States. It is also located less than 250 miles from Canada, an important neighbor and trading partner of the United States. Kentucky borders the Mississippi River and the Ohio River, which are important to trade.

A Southeast State

"In the Southeast" is another way to describe Kentucky's relative location. Kentucky is one of the 13 states that make up the **Southeast** region of the United States. A **region** is an area with at least one feature that makes it different from other areas. All the states in the Southeast are located in the southeastern part of the United States.

Within the Southeast, Kentucky is part of a smaller region called the **Inland South**. The four states in this region are the only Southeast states that do not border the ocean.

READING CHECK ☼ **MAIN IDEA AND DETAILS**
Which states border Kentucky?

Kentucky and United States Regions

DIAGRAM What is Kentucky's location in relation to the Midwest region?

WEST

MIDWEST

NORTHEAST

SOUTHWEST

SOUTHEAST

KENTUCKY

▶ **THE LAND BETWEEN THE LAKES** is the name given to the land between Lake Barkley and Kentucky Lake. It is home to much wildlife, including the White-Tailed Deer (right).

Physical Regions

People divide places into regions to make them easier to study and understand. Any characteristic, or feature, can be used to define a region.

Physical Characteristics

Many regions are defined by **physical characteristics**, or features formed by nature. These features include such things as rivers, lakes, mountains, and forests.

Kentucky has a great variety of physical features. The north-central part of the state is made up of flat or rolling grasslands. Much of eastern Kentucky, however, is mountainous.

Kentucky has more than 1,000 miles of rivers. The Ohio River forms the entire northern border of Kentucky, while the Mississippi forms the western border. The Cumberland and many other rivers flow through the state.

Kentucky's many lakes are all human-made reservoirs. The largest is Lake Cumberland, in the southern part of the state. Farther west lie Lake Barkley and Kentucky Lake.

Weather and climate can define a physical region, too. In general, Kentucky has a mild climate. Winters tend to be cool, while summers are hot. The state gets plenty of rain, especially in spring. Kentucky's mountainous areas get lots of snow.

READING CHECK ⚙ **MAIN IDEA AND DETAILS**
What are some physical characteristics that can define a region?

▶ **LOUISVILLE** is located along the Ohio River. It was a busy port in 1876 (left) and still is today (above).

People and Regions

Other regions are defined by their **human characteristics**, or features created by people. These features include cities, farms, roads, businesses, languages, and religions.

Patterns of Settlement

In some cases, human features depend on physical features. For example, people need fresh water to live. As a result, most early settlers in Kentucky built their homes near rivers, streams, and springs.

Rivers also provided an easy way to travel. Instead of hauling their goods over rough land, settlers could load boats and travel by water to their new home in Kentucky. Once there, they used the rivers as trade routes.

Today, many of Kentucky's cities are located along waterways. For example, Louisville, Kentucky's largest city, grew up along the Ohio River. The state capital, Frankfort, was founded on the Kentucky River.

Most early settlers were farmers. As a result, they chose to live in places with flat land, rich soil, and plenty of rain. This led them to settle in valleys rather than mountains.

However, the mountains offer resources that have attracted settlers. Hundreds of years ago, hunters and trappers came to the mountains for the deer, beavers, and other wildlife.

Later, logging companies moved into the area to harvest the forests of pine, oak, and other trees. By the 1900s, many towns had grown around the coal mines in the mountains.

Much of Kentucky's coal is mined in the mountains of eastern Kentucky. This area of Kentucky is a part of **Appalachia**, a region in and around the southern Appalachian Mountains. Appalachia is defined by its land and by the way of life of its people. It has a rich history of storytelling and music.

READING CHECK ⚆**MAIN IDEA AND DETAILS**
Why did many early settlers in Kentucky settle along rivers?

❱ **MOUNTAINS** People have always admired the beautiful scenery in the mountains of eastern Kentucky.

Summary

Kentucky is located in the southeastern part of the United States. The state has a mild climate, rich farmlands, mountains, and many rivers and lakes. These physical characteristics affected where people settled in the state and where cities grew.

REVIEW

1. **WHAT TO KNOW** Where is Kentucky, and what is important about its location?

2. **VOCABULARY** How are **physical characteristics** different from **human characteristics**?

3. **GEOGRAPHY** Why did more people in the past settle in Kentucky's valleys than in its mountains?

4. **CRITICAL THINKING** Kentucky is a Southeast state and an Inland South state. How do these two region names describe Kentucky's geography?

5. **DRAW A MAP** Draw an outline map of Kentucky, showing where other states border it. Label each of those states.

6. **MAIN IDEA AND DETAILS** On a separate sheet of paper, copy and complete the graphic organizer below.

Main Idea
There are several ways to describe Kentucky's location.

Details

Map and Globe Skills

Use Latitude and Longitude

Why It Matters By stating latitude and longitude, you can describe the **absolute location**, or exact location, of a place.

❯ LEARN

Lines of latitude and longitude cross to form a grid over a map or globe. To describe a place's absolute location, you name the line of latitude and line of longitude closest to it.

Lines of latitude run east and west on a map or globe. The equator is a line of latitude. Find the equator on Map A. It is marked 0°, or zero degrees. All other lines of latitude are measured in degrees north or south from the equator.

Lines of longitude run north and south on a map or globe. The **prime meridian** is a line of longitude. Find the prime meridian on Map A. Like the equator, it is marked 0°. All other lines of longitude are measured in degrees east or west from the prime meridian.

Map A: Latitude and Longitude

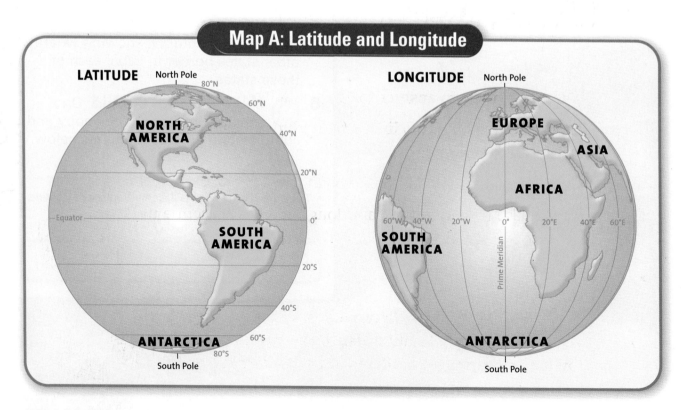

14 ▪ Unit 1

The Mississippi Embayment Region

The Mississippi Embayment Region is also known as the Jackson Purchase Region. It covers the western corner of Kentucky. It has the lowest lands and the only swamps in Kentucky. Plains are the main landform there.

The Mississippi Embayment is bordered by the Ohio, Mississippi, and Tennessee Rivers. In the past, these rivers flooded often, leaving rich soil behind. People once grew a lot of cotton there. Now, soybeans are the most important crop.

READING CHECK Ŏ**MAIN IDEA AND DETAILS**
What landform covers most of the Mississippi Embayment Region?

▶ **SWAMPLAND** covers parts of the Mississippi Embayment Region and is home to many forms of wildlife.

Summary

Each of Kentucky's six natural regions is defined by its unique physical characteristics. Some have mountains. Others have plains. Some regions have coal or forests. Others are good for farming or raising animals.

REVIEW

1. **WHAT TO KNOW** What is unique about each of Kentucky's natural regions?

2. **VOCABULARY** Use the word **erosion** in a sentence that describes how the Knobs Region was formed.

3. **GEOGRAPHY** Which two regions have the highest and the lowest lands in Kentucky?

4. **CRITICAL THINKING** In which natural region of Kentucky do you live? What are some of the physical features near your home that are common in this region?

5. **CREATE A TRAVEL POSTER** Make a travel poster showing physical features in one of Kentucky's natural regions.

6. **MAIN IDEA AND DETAILS** On a separate sheet of paper, copy and complete the graphic organizer below.

Main Idea
Geographers divide Kentucky into six natural regions.

Details					

People and Resources

VOCABULARY

natural resource p. 25
product p. 25
modify p. 26
mineral p. 26
fossil fuel p. 26
population p. 28
limited resource p. 29
scarcity p. 29

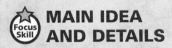 **MAIN IDEA AND DETAILS**

Main Idea

Details

YOU ARE THERE Your hands are covered with soil. You rinse them with the hose. "Great soil! It's going to be a good year for the garden," you say to your mother. "Let's go buy seeds. I'll make a list." Mom hands you a pencil and takes out her car keys.

You start to think about how many of nature's gifts you depend on every day. You can name soil, water, seeds, wood for the pencil, and gas for the car. You wonder how many more you can think of on the way to buy seeds.

BEANS
KENTUCKY WONDER

➤ **GARDENING** Kentucky has excellent soil for planting gardens.

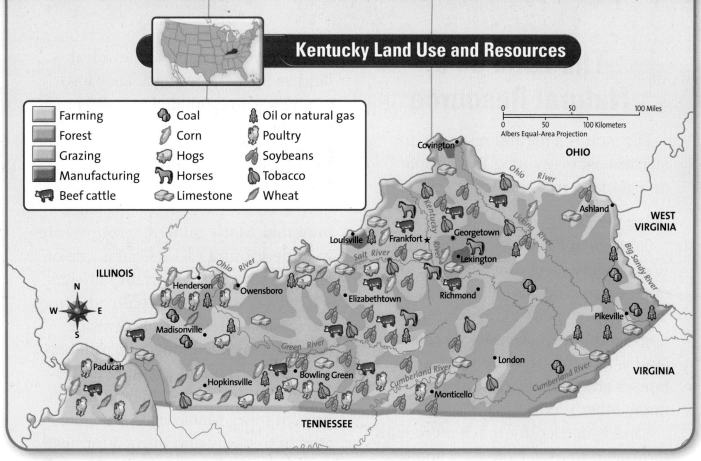

Kentucky Land Use and Resources

Legend:
- Farming
- Forest
- Grazing
- Manufacturing
- Beef cattle
- Coal
- Corn
- Hogs
- Horses
- Limestone
- Oil or natural gas
- Poultry
- Soybeans
- Tobacco
- Wheat

0   50   100 Miles
0   50   100 Kilometers
Albers Equal-Area Projection

MAP SKILL HUMAN-ENVIRONMENT INTERACTIONS Kentucky is rich in natural resources. How is land used in your area of the state?

Natural Resources

Kentucky is rich in natural resources. A **natural resource** is something found in nature that people can use. Water, soil, and even air are natural resources. Wood is a natural resource, too, as are sand, iron, limestone, and coal—all things found in Kentucky.

How We Use Them

People use natural resources in many ways. Some are usable just as they are found. People breathe the air and drink the water. They eat garden vegetables and wild blackberries.

Other natural resources must be changed before they are used.

For example, stone is an important natural resource in Kentucky. Most of this stone is not used in its natural state. Much of the stone is crushed to just the right size so that it can be used to build roads.

Natural resources are needed to make most products. A **product** is something that people make or grow, usually to sell. To make pencils, for example, someone must first chop down a tree to get wood. Blackberries grow wild in the state, but people must change them to make a jar of blackberry jam.

READING CHECK ⟲ MAIN IDEA AND DETAILS
In what different ways do people use natural resources?

The Land as a Natural Resource

The land is a natural resource. In fact, almost everything that people do uses land in some way.

Using the Land

Farmers in Kentucky use the land to grow corn, soybeans, tobacco, and other crops. The land also produces the food they need to raise cattle, hogs, and horses. Kentucky's forested land is a source of wood used to build houses and to make furniture and many other products.

Land is needed for much more than farms and forests. Houses, schools, stores, and factories are built on land. So are railroads and highways.

People **modify**, or change, the land just as they change other natural resources. For example, they clear land so it can be farmed. They also cut through mountains to build roads and tunnels.

Underground Resources

Some natural resources are found in rocks. These resources are called **minerals**. Many mineral resources are in underground rocks. Coal is one of Kentucky's most important minerals.

Coal, oil, and natural gas come from the fossils, or remains of plants or animals that lived long ago. Millions of years of heat and pressure underground have changed them into their present form. Materials that are created in this way and burned for heat or energy are called **fossil fuels**.

`READING CHECK` ŎMAIN IDEA AND DETAILS
What are some ways people modify their environment to meet their needs?

▶ **FARMERS** use Kentucky's land to raise animals and grow many crops, such as tobacco (below).

Corn

Soybeans

Hogs

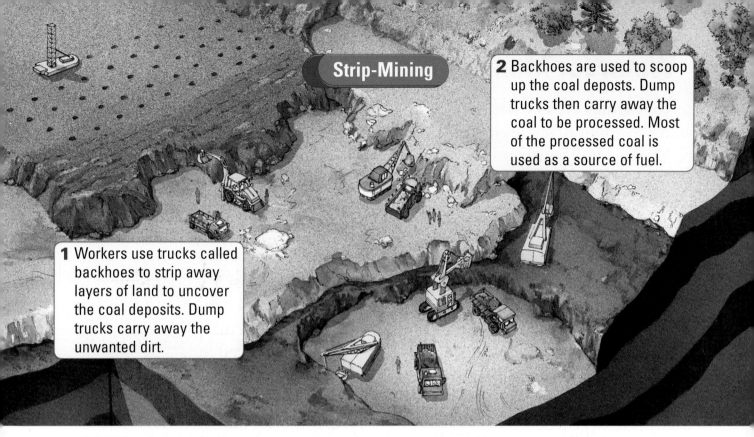

Strip-Mining

1 Workers use trucks called backhoes to strip away layers of land to uncover the coal deposits. Dump trucks carry away the unwanted dirt.

2 Backhoes are used to scoop up the coal deposts. Dump trucks then carry away the coal to be processed. Most of the processed coal is used as a source of fuel.

ILLUSTRATION Strip-mining is one way to get coal from the land. What do you think is done with the dirt that is taken away?

Coal

Kentucky is the third-largest producer of coal in the United States. Coal mined in the state is sold for billions of dollars each year.

Mining Coal

Coal is mined in two ways. One kind of mining is done underground. The coal is dug up and taken away. The other kind involves stripping off the top of the land to get the coal.

Strip-mining removes trees and soil and changes the look of the land. Afterward, it is difficult to get trees and plants to grow as they did before.

Today, people understand how important the land is. In fact, the law now states that after mining, the land must be reclaimed, or changed back to a usable form. Most land that is strip-mined is reclaimed as flat land. This land can be used for farming or other human use.

Using Coal

Most of Kentucky's coal is used to produce electricity. Nearly all of the state's electricity comes from coal. The coal is burned to heat water, which creates steam. The steam runs machinery that creates electricity.

However, smoke from burning coal makes the air unhealthy to breathe. There are ways to make the burning of coal cleaner. Still, more work needs to be done to protect our air—another precious natural resource.

READING CHECK ☉**MAIN IDEA AND DETAILS**
What are the two main methods of mining coal?

Water for Many Uses

No resource is more necessary than water. Without it, life itself would be impossible. There is probably no resource that has more uses than water.

Kentucky's Water

Kentucky is lucky to have many sources of water. Its rivers alone satisfy a variety of needs. The rivers supply drinking water for cities. They enable boats to transport people and goods from one place to another. They power machinery that produces electricity. They provide water for farms to grow food. They are a place for fishing and swimming. Kentucky's many lakes also supply water for drinking, making electricity, and recreation.

Caring for Our Water

Long ago, Kentucky had few people. The water they used went back to the streams it had come from or went underground.

Since then, the **population**, or the number of people, in Kentucky has grown. Most of these people use a lot of water every day.

When we use water, it still goes back into nature. Yet there are so many of us now that our washing machines, factories, farms, and mines make the water dirty and sometimes poisonous. Keeping our water clean is one of the most important challenges we face together in the coming years.

READING CHECK Ŏ **MAIN IDEA AND DETAILS**
What are some ways in which people in Kentucky use water?

How Much Water?

USE	AMOUNT
Brushing teeth	1 to 2 gallons
Flushing a toilet	5 to 7 gallons
Running a dishwasher	9 to 12 gallons
Taking a shower	15 to 30 gallons
Washing dishes by hand	20 to 30 gallons

GRAPH Each person in the United States uses an average of about 120 gallons of water a day. Some farmers in Kentucky use sprinkler systems to water their crops. About how much water does a person use to take a shower?

Conserving Natural Resources

In recent years, many Kentuckians have made the decision to change their habits in order to conserve, or use wisely, natural resources. For example, they know that coal is a **limited resource**—one that will run out someday. They try to use less electricity, since coal is used to make it.

When people want more of a resource than what is available, the problem of **scarcity** occurs. This problem could happen more in the future if people do not use limited resources wisely.

READING CHECK ⭘**MAIN IDEA AND DETAILS**
What is the problem of scarcity?

Summary

Kentucky has water, soil, trees, coal, and other natural resources. People in the state depend on these resources to live and to get products they want. For this reason, many people in Kentucky conserve their natural resources and use them wisely.

REVIEW

1. **WHAT TO KNOW** How does human activity affect natural resources?

2. **VOCABULARY** Define the term **limited resource**, and give an example of one.

3. **HISTORY** How has Kentucky's population changed since its early days?

4. **CRITICAL THINKING** Gasoline is a limited resource. How could we improve the way it is used?

5. **WRITE A RADIO COMMERCIAL** Write a 30-second radio commercial. Your goal is to persuade people to put on their house special windows that will keep the heat in better during the winter.

6. **MAIN IDEA AND DETAILS** On a separate sheet of paper, copy and complete the graphic organizer below.

Main Idea

Water is a very important resource.

Details

READ ABOUT

Mammoth Cave National Park

A PARK RANGER will lead these visitors through the mouth of the cave.

Mammoth Cave is the largest known cave system in the world. Over 340 miles of passages snake through the limestone. Because of its beauty and uniqueness, Mammoth Cave was made a national park in 1941.

The cave is home to many beautiful and unique rock formations. Visitors also come to meet the strange animals that live in the cave's darkness.

Above the cave, visitors also enjoy hundreds of acres of beautiful Kentucky scenery. There, visitors can find boat tours and nature trails—all a part of Mammoth Cave National Park.

FIND

Mammoth Cave National Park

KENTUCKY

CATHEDRAL DOMES

"RUINS OF KARNAK"

THE GREEN RIVER

FIRE PINK FLOWER

SALAMANDER

A VIRTUAL TOUR

GO
ONLINE For more resources go to
www.harcourtschool.com/ss1

Time

12,000 YEARS AGO   1,000 YEARS AGO

About 12,000 years ago
People arrive in Kentucky

About 3,000 years ago
Native Kentuckians start growing corn and beans

About 1,000 years ago
Mississippians build mounds in Kentucky

WHAT TO KNOW
How did the early people of Kentucky change their ways of life as their environment changed?

VOCABULARY
glacier p. 33

ancestor p. 33

extinct p. 34

barter p. 34

agriculture p. 35

permanent p. 35

earthworks p. 36

ceremony p. 37

PEOPLE
Paleo-Indians

Archaic Indians

Adena

Mississippians

Mound Builders

PLACES
Great Lakes

Gulf of Mexico

Ohio River

Mississippi Valley

Wickliffe Mounds

MAIN IDEA AND DETAILS

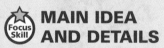

Main Idea

Details

Early People of Kentucky

YOU ARE THERE

The hunter next to you raises his arm slowly and points to a spot in the distance. You look where he is pointing. Down the hill, by the watering hole, stands a mammoth. For the first time in weeks, you will have a source of meat. This animal will feed all of you for days. Its hide will provide warmth and shelter for the winter. You move slowly toward it, spear in hand.

Long, Long Ago

About 12,000 years ago, small groups of hunters reached what is now Kentucky. They were the first people to interact with Kentucky's environment.

Ice Ages

In the past, Earth had long periods of cold, known as Ice Ages. **Glaciers**, or fields of ice, covered large areas of Earth, including Kentucky.

Much of Earth's water was frozen in the glaciers. So much water was taken up by the glaciers that less water was left in the oceans. At times, this exposed a "bridge" of dry land between Asia and North America.

The Paleo-Indians

Many scientists think people first reached North America from Asia by crossing that land bridge. Those early people are now called **Paleo-Indians**.

However, many present-day Native Americans believe that their people have always lived in the Americas.

Over thousands of years, the Paleo-Indians spread throughout North and South America. They were the **ancestors**, or early family members, of present-day Native Americans, also called American Indians.

When Paleo-Indians came to Kentucky, glaciers lay just to the north. Kentucky was colder than it is now.

Kentucky's Paleo-Indians followed herds of animals from place to place. They used spears with stone points to hunt huge mastodons and woolly mammoths. They probably gathered some wild plants for food, too.

READING CHECK ŎMAIN IDEA AND DETAILS
How did Paleo-Indians get most of their food?

MAP SKILL

MOVEMENT The first people to reach North America were likely nomads. A nomad is a person who keeps moving from place to place. In which general direction did early people travel from Asia to reach what is now Kentucky?

LAND ROUTES OF EARLY PEOPLE

ASIA

ARCTIC OCEAN

EUROPE

Bering Strait

NORTH AMERICA

ATLANTIC OCEAN

Tropic of Cancer

40°N

PACIFIC OCEAN

0°

Equator

SOUTH AMERICA

Tropic of Capricorn

100°W

40°S

Land
Glacier
Sea ice
Route

▶ **HUNTING** When large animals died out, early people began hunting smaller animals, such as elk, deer, and rabbits.

New Ways of Life

Over time, the climate became warmer and drier. This caused people to start developing new ways of life about 10,000 years ago. The people who lived during this period are now called **Archaic** (ar•KAY•ik) **Indians**.

New Foods

As the climate changed, many of the plants that the large animals ate stopped growing. This may be one reason why those animals became **extinct**, or died out.

With no more large animals to hunt, people had to find new ways to get food. They started fishing more. They hunted smaller animals, such as deer, rabbits, and birds. They gathered more wild plants, nuts, and berries. In time, they learned where the best places were to find food during each season.

Trade and Tools

The Archaic Indians in Kentucky used boats on rivers to travel long distances to **barter**, or trade things. They got copper from the **Great Lakes** region and shells from the **Gulf of Mexico**. They used these materials to make better tools and weapons.

The Archaic Indians also used bones and antlers to make fishhooks, needles, and drilling tools. They learned to make baskets by weaving plant fibers. Some baskets were woven so tightly that they could hold water!

READING CHECK **COMPARE AND CONTRAST**
How was the life of the Archaic Indians different from that of the Paleo-Indians?

More Changes

By the end of the Archaic period, life for Native Americans changed even more. They started farming and living in villages.

Growing Food

About 3,000 years ago, Native Americans in Kentucky began to grow squash, sunflowers, and other plants. At about the same time, people from other regions brought corn and beans to Kentucky. People in Kentucky began to grow these crops, too.

Agriculture, or farming, required clearing the land. That involved a lot of work. It made little sense to move to another place after only one harvest. If people did that, they would have to start over and clear new land. Instead, they stayed and planted crops again on the same land. In addition, people had to stay close by to care for and protect the crops.

Settling Down

As a result of farming, Native Americans started building **permanent**, or long-lasting, shelters and staying in one place. They still went out hunting, sometimes for days. When the hunt was over, though, they returned home. In time, they formed villages.

Most villages in Kentucky were built along rivers and streams. Sometimes, native peoples who did not farm attacked the villages to get the food that was stored there. Some villagers built walls for protection against such attacks.

READING CHECK ☼**MAIN IDEA AND DETAILS**
How did Native Americans change the land to meet their needs?

▶ **EARLY FARMING** Men used large sticks to break up the soil, women used hoes to make furrows, and then smaller sticks were used to make holes in which the seeds were planted.

The Cherokee

The **Cherokee** hunted and later settled in the mountain valleys of southeastern Kentucky. They built villages along rivers.

Village Life

Cherokee villages were built around a central square with a council house that was large and circle-shaped. The council house was used for religious ceremonies and sometimes sat on top of an earthen mound.

Most Cherokee had two houses. Winter houses were small, round structures. Dirt covered the frame to hold in heat. Summer houses were larger and box-shaped. They had grass or clay walls and roofs made of bark.

Neither kind of house had separate rooms. An extended family shared one open space around a fire. When a couple got married, they made their home with the woman's family. When asked what family they belonged to, the Cherokee gave their mother's family name.

Cherokee women and men specialized (SPEH•shuh•lyzd) in their work. To **specialize** is to work at one kind of job and learn to do it well. Cherokee women grew crops, such as corn and squash. Men brought food from outside the village by hunting and by gathering plants.

READING CHECK ☿**MAIN IDEA AND DETAILS**
In what kinds of jobs did Cherokee men and women specialize?

Children IN HISTORY

Cherokee Children

Cherokee children of the past had less time for play than most American children do today. Boys went hunting and fishing with their fathers. Girls helped their mothers gather and grow food and cook meals.

Cherokee children did have toys and play games, however. In fact, they played some of the same games that children play today. These include tag, hide-and-seek, and racing games.

Teenage boys learned to play a ball game known today as lacrosse. Players used the sticks with nets on one end to catch a ball made of deerskin. Cherokee groups sometimes played this game to settle a conflict.

Make It Relevant **What kind of games do you like to play?**

▶ A CHICKASAW VILLAGE The Chickasaw lived in villages in the Mississippi Embayment Region. How might living in large villages have protected the Chickasaw from their enemies?

The Chickasaw

A small number of **Chickasaw** lived in the Mississippi Embayment Region of western Kentucky. They were known as fierce warriors.

Warriors

The Chickasaw protected their land forcefully. They also attacked neighboring tribes, such as the Choctaw and the Creek. These three tribes spoke similar languages.

Before an attack, a Chickasaw warrior shaved most of his hair and applied war paint. Chickasaw men and women often had several tattoos. Many also had flattened foreheads. This was the result of pressure applied when they were infants. The Chickasaw thought flat foreheads were attractive.

Similarities and Differences

Like many other Native Americans, the Chickasaw people believed in a god who lived in the sky and created all the world's light, warmth, and life. As in the Cherokee tribe, a Chickasaw belonged to his or her mother's family.

Chickasaw houses were nearly identical to those of the Cherokee. However, Chickasaw villages changed in size depending on whether the time was one of war or one of peace. In times of peace, Chickasaw villages usually spread out. In times of war, the houses and buildings were grouped closely together to make them easier to defend during an attack.

READING CHECK ☼MAIN IDEA AND DETAILS
Where in Kentucky did the Chickasaw live?

The Shawnee

The **Shawnee** lived along the Ohio River and in the central part of what is now Kentucky. They were farming people. They grew corn and squash in the fertile soil that was plentiful where they lived.

Trading and Hunting

The Ohio River and other waterways also provided a good way to travel and trade. The Shawnee used dugout canoes to travel on rivers. They made the canoes by hollowing out large tree trunks. There were many forests along the river, so the Shawnee had plenty of trunks to use.

In the forests, Shawnee men used arrows and spears to hunt deer, turkeys, and other small animals. They also used spears and nets to catch bass, trout, and other fish in the Ohio River and smaller streams. Shawnee women grew crops, gathered firewood, and cooked meals.

Community Life

Shawnee villages had as many as 100 houses. These were round, bark-covered shelters called **wigwams**. Most villages also had a large, special building in which the community could gather and discuss things.

Unlike some other tribes, Shawnee families were grouped around the men's families rather than the women's families. Different families had different responsibilities. Some were warriors, others were healers, and still others led religious activities.

READING CHECK Ŏ **MAIN IDEA AND DETAILS**
What benefits did the Shawnee find in living near the Ohio River?

▶ **A SHAWNEE VILLAGE** The Shawnee once had villages in the Bluegrass Region and depended on the natural resources there.

The Iroquois and Other Groups

Many Native Americans who did not live in Kentucky used the area as hunting grounds. Among them were the Wyandot, the Delaware, and the Iroquois. The **Iroquois** were a group of tribes that lived in what is now the state of New York.

Strength in Unity

For many years, the Iroquois fought with each other and with neighboring tribes. Many of the fights were over control of the hunting grounds. To stop the fighting, five Iroquois tribes united. **Deganawida** was an Iroquois leader who helped unite the tribes.

Though each tribe continued to rule itself, together they made decisions about matters that affected all the tribes. One such matter was war.

Village Life

The Iroquois lived in villages. Their homes were called **longhouses**. The frame of a longhouse was built by bending poles made from young trees. Then the frame was covered with bark. As many as 20 families might live in one longhouse.

Most Iroquois villages were surrounded by a wall made of tall wooden poles. Outside the walls, Iroquois women grew corn, beans, and squash. They called these crops the Three Sisters because all three were planted in the same field.

READING CHECK ☼ **MAIN IDEA AND DETAILS**
What natural resources did the Iroquois use to build their homes and villages?

Learning from the Past

Early Native Americans left no written record of their experiences to describe how they lived. Even so, people who study the distant past have ways to learn about customs, tools, food, and beliefs of people long ago.

Artifacts

Much of what we know about Native Americans in Kentucky comes from the artifacts (AR•tih•fakts) they left behind. An **artifact** is an object made by people in the past.

From artifacts, such as spear points or arrow tips, scientists can figure out how people hunted or fought. Hoes, needles, and other tools can give clues about how people grew food or made their clothes. Artifacts made from animal bones can show whether people had dogs or what kind of meat they ate.

Storytelling

Another way of learning about Native American ways of life is to study their stories, songs, and teachings that have been passed down for many years. Like people everywhere, Native Americans in Kentucky wondered about the world around them. They created stories to explain

▶ ARTIFACTS University science students search a site where Native Americans lived long ago. Arrowheads and jewelry made from shells and beads are a few of the artifacts they might find.

➤ **STORYTELLERS** pass Native American history and beliefs on to the next generation.

how people and everything in the world came to be. Kentucky's Native Americans also told stories about their tribe's history and beliefs.

Children listened carefully as their elders repeated these stories. In time, they learned the stories by heart and passed them on to their own children. Stories that are handed down over time are called **legends**.

The Cherokee had many legends. Today, these legends are being written down for all to share. **Murv Jacob** draws pictures for books that tell Cherokee legends. Jacob's ancestors were Kentucky Cherokee. One of Jacob's books tells a legend about why rabbits have short tails.

READING CHECK ŎMAIN IDEA AND DETAILS
Where does our knowledge about early Native American tribes come from?

Summary

The Cherokee, Chickasaw, Shawnee, and Iroquois were Native American tribes that lived, farmed, or hunted in Kentucky. Each group used natural resources. Each had its own culture. Most passed down their history and culture through stories.

REVIEW

1. **WHAT TO KNOW** How did Native Americans in Kentucky use natural resources to meet their needs?

2. **VOCABULARY** What is an example of an **artifact**, and what might it tell you about the past?

3. **CULTURE** How did the early Native Americans pass down their history and beliefs?

4. **CRITICAL THINKING** How do you think farming allowed Native Americans to specialize in other tasks?

5. **WRITE A STORY** Write a legend that explains a natural event such as a blizzard or a thunderstorm.

6. **MAIN IDEA AND DETAILS** On a separate sheet of paper, copy and complete the graphic organizer below.

Main Idea

Native Americans in Kentucky grew many of the same crops.

Details

Biographies

Trustworthiness
Respect
Responsibility
Fairness
Caring
Patriotism

Native American Leaders

Many groups of Native Americans lived in North America before the Europeans arrived. Although few Native Americans lived in Kentucky year-round, many tribes traveled through it to hunt and fish. When the Europeans came, each Native American group had to decide for itself how to treat the newcomers.

Cornstalk was an important Shawnee chief when Europeans first began to settle in Kentucky. He saw that the Europeans often treated the Shawnee unfairly and that they were claiming lands where the Shawnee had always lived and hunted. Cornstalk decided that his people had to fight. The Shawnee and other Native American tribes fought against the colonial soldiers in Lord Dunmore's War. In this terrible war, many Native Americans and colonists died. Cornstalk felt responsible for his people. He decided to turn against violence. He believed the Shawnee would be safer if they made peace with the Europeans.

Cornstalk

About 1727–1777
Character Trait: Responsibility

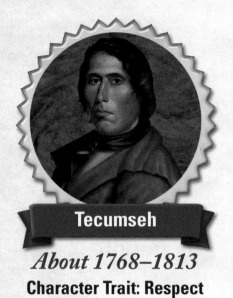

Tecumseh

About 1768–1813

Character Trait: Respect

Tecumseh was a Shawnee leader. He, too, wanted to stop Europeans from controlling the lands of his ancestors. Tecumseh tried to get the Native American tribes to fight against the Europeans to preserve their way of life. He thought his people should stop wearing European clothes and stop using European tools and weapons. Shortly before his death in battle, Tecumseh asked his Native American forces to have mercy on a group of captured Kentucky soldiers. He believed that even his enemies deserved to be treated with respect.

Sequoyah was from the Cherokee tribe. He invented a system of writing for his people. In the past, the Cherokee remembered their history through storytelling. With Sequoyah's alphabet, the Cherokee could write it down. Soon they were printing their own newspapers and writing their own books. Sequoyah spent most of his life traveling through the United States. When he found groups of Cherokee, he would teach them about his alphabet. He cared about his people and wanted them to be able to write down their thoughts and beliefs in their own language.

Sequoyah

About 1760–1843

Character Trait: Caring

Why Character Counts

1. How did Cornstalk demonstrate responsibility?

2. In what way did Tecumseh show respect?

3. How did Sequoyah show he cared for his people?

  For more resources, go to
www.harcourtschool.com/ss1

Review and Test Prep

THE BIG IDEA

Geography People in Kentucky have always interacted with their environment and been affected by it.

Reading Comprehension and Vocabulary

Kentucky's Geography and Early People

Kentucky is in the Northern Hemisphere and in the Western Hemisphere. It is on the continent of North America and in the Southeast region of the United States. Kentucky's physical characteristics include grass-lands, mountains, forests, rivers, and lakes.

Kentucky is divided into six natural regions. They are the Bluegrass, the Knobs, the Eastern Kentucky Coal Field, the Mississippian Plateau, the Western Kentucky Coal Field, and the Mississippi Embayment.

The state is rich in natural resources. They include land, minerals, and water.

Kentucky's earliest people were hunters and gatherers who arrived about 12,000 years ago. About 3,000 years ago, people in Kentucky began to grow crops and build villages. The Adena and the Mississippians were Mound Builders.

In time, Native Americans developed different cultures and tribes. The Cherokee, the Chickasaw, and the Shawnee lived in different parts of Kentucky.

Read the summary above. Then answer the questions that follow.

1. In which region of the United States is Kentucky located?
   A the West
   B the Southeast
   C the Southwest
   D the Northeast

2. What is a natural resource?
   A something that will run out someday
   B something that is burned for heat or energy
   C something that people make or grow and then sell
   D something found in nature that people can use

3. What happened about 3,000 years ago?
   A The first people came to Kentucky.
   B People began to farm in Kentucky.
   C The Mound Builders disappeared.
   D Native Americans split into tribes.

4. What is culture?
   A a group's ways of life
   B a story handed down over time
   C a shelter built by Native Americans
   D an object made by people in the past

Answer these questions.

5. What is Kentucky's location relative to Canada?

6. In what areas of Kentucky did most early settlers choose to live?

7. In what ways do Kentucky farmers use the land as a natural resource?

8. What is one way in which people in present-day Kentucky modify the land?

9. How did the lives of early people in Kentucky change when large animals became extinct?

10. What crops did the Shawnee grow?

Write the letter of the best choice.

11. Which of the following is a human characteristic of Appalachia?
    A forests
    B music
    C mountains
    D rivers

12. Which physical characteristic is found in the Mississippi Embayment Region?
    A mountains
    B deserts
    C swamps
    D dunes

13. Who were Kentucky's earliest people?
    A the Archaic Indians
    B the Paleo-Indians
    C the Mississippians
    D the Chickasaw

14. Which of the following did early people in Kentucky get by bartering?
    A bones
    B antlers
    C copper
    D plants

 Critical Thinking

15. How did physical characteristics affect patterns of settlement in Kentucky?

16. In what ways were Native American ways of life alike and different from how people live in Kentucky today?

 Skills

Use Latitude and Longitude

Use the map on page 15 to answer this question

17. Between which two lines of longitude does most of the Kentucky River run?

OPEN-RESPONSE

Writing Task 1

Situation: You just took a trip through all six of Kentucky's natural regions.

Writing Task: Write a letter to your pen pal telling him or her about the physical and human characteristics in each of the regions. Also explain what is similar and what is different about each region.

Writing Task 2

Situation: You are the first explorer from Europe to visit Native Americans in Kentucky. You have traveled all over and witnessed how the people live.

Writing Task: Write a journal entry that compares the different cultures you encountered in your travels. Make sure to describe how each culture uses natural resources to meet its needs.

 For more resources, go to
www.harcourtschool.com/ss1

Fun with Social Studies

KENTUCKY

Shawnee
Mound Builders
Atlantic Ocean
Agriculture
Rocky Mts.
Desert
Coal Mines
Appalachian Mts.
Chickasaw

Oops!

Which three labels don't belong anywhere on the Kentucky bulletin board?

Riddle Silliness

Figure out what letter each number stands for, and you'll know the answer to the riddle!

VOCABULARY

The _ _ 1 _ _ _ _ divides Earth into the Northern and Southern Hemispheres.

2 _ _ _ _ _ _ _ are fields of ice.

The slow wearing away of Earth's surface by wind or water is called _ _ _ 3 _ _ _ .

To trade one item for another is to 4 _ _ _ _ _ .

Coal, oil and natural gas are examples of _ _ _ _ _ _ _ _ 5 _ _ .

Water that falls to Earth's surface as rain, sleet, hail, or snow is _ _ _ _ _ _ _ _ 6 _ _ _ _ .

To 7 _ _ _ _ _ _ _ _ _ is to work at one kind of job and learn to do it well.

A resource that is limited is said to be _ _ _ 8 _ _ .

A story that is handed down over time is called a 9 _ _ _ _ _ .

Why did the silly man from Kentucky tell sad stories to the plants in his yard?
He wanted 491528637

Europeans Settle Kentucky

 Start with the Standards

Kentucky Core Content for Assessment

SS-04-1.3.1 Students will identify the basic principles of democracy found in Kentucky's Constitution and explain why they are important to citizens today.

SS-04-2.1.1 Students will identify early cultures in Kentucky and explain their similarities and differences.

SS-04-2.3.1 Students will describe various forms of interactions that occurred during the early settlement of Kentucky between diverse groups.

SS-04-4.1.3 Students will describe how different factors influence where human activities were/are located in Kentucky.

SS-04-4.3.1 Students will describe patterns of human settlement in regions of Kentucky and explain how these patterns were/are influenced by physical characteristics.

SS-04-4.4.1 Students will explain and give examples of how people adapted to/modified the physical environment to meet their needs during the history of Kentucky and explain its impact on the environment today.

SS-04-4.4.2 Students will describe how the physical environment both promoted and restricted human activities during the early settlement of Kentucky.

SS-04-5.1.1 Students will use a variety of primary and secondary sources to describe significant events in the history of Kentucky and interpret different perspectives.

SS-04-5.2.2 Students will identify and compare the cultures of diverse groups and explain why people explored and settled Kentucky.

SS-04-5.2.3 Students will compare change over time in communication, technology, transportation and education in Kentucky.

The Big Idea

Exploration and Settlement

The exploration and settlement of Kentucky led to interaction between diverse peoples.

What to Know

✓ What attracted European explorers to Kentucky?

✓ What difficulties did the first European settlers in Kentucky face?

✓ What part did Kentucky play in the American Revolution?

✓ What process led to Kentucky becoming its own state?

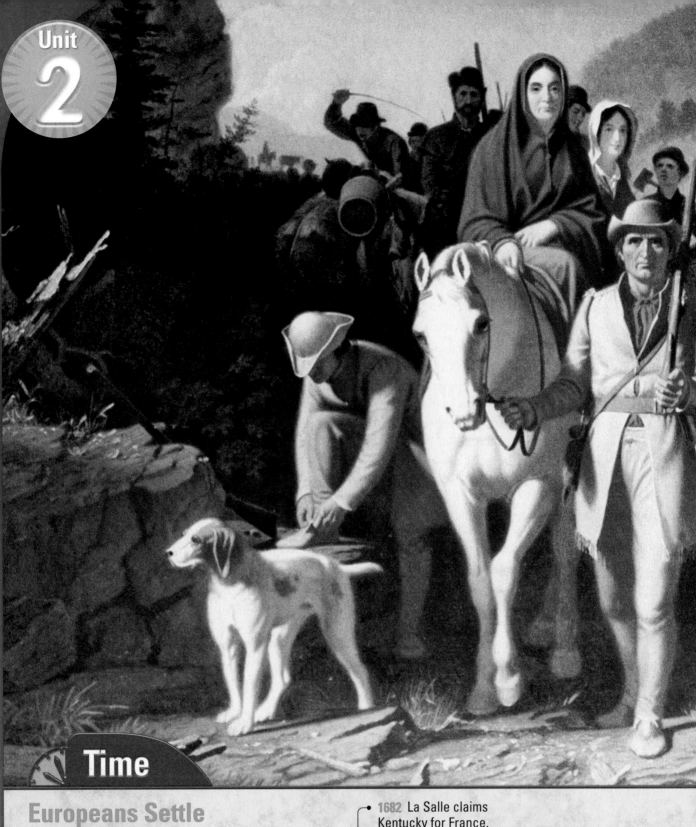

Time

Europeans Settle Kentucky

● **1682** La Salle claims Kentucky for France, p. 62

1650

1700

At the Same Time

 1620 The Pilgrims land in what is now Massachusetts

 1695 The Spanish finish building the Castillo de San Marcos in St Augustine, Florida

Europeans Settle Kentucky

1750 Dr. Thomas Walker finds the Cumberland Gap, p. 64

1775 Daniel Boone begins building Boonesborough, p. 73

1792 Kentucky becomes a state, p. 93

1750

1800

1754 The French and Indian War begins

1776 The 13 English colonies declare their independence

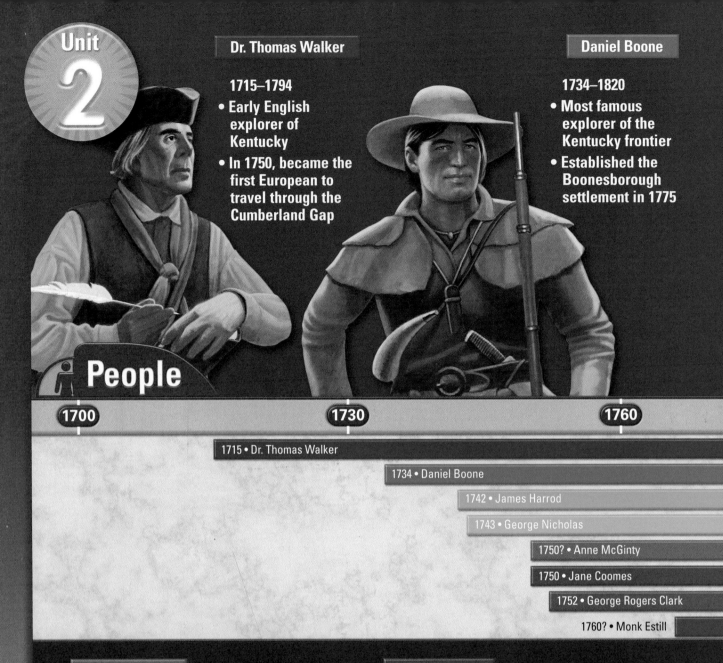

Dr. Thomas Walker

1715–1794
- Early English explorer of Kentucky
- In 1750, became the first European to travel through the Cumberland Gap

Daniel Boone

1734–1820
- Most famous explorer of the Kentucky frontier
- Established the Boonesborough settlement in 1775

 People

1700		1730		1760

1715 • Dr. Thomas Walker

1734 • Daniel Boone

1742 • James Harrod

1743 • George Nicholas

1750? • Anne McGinty

1750 • Jane Coomes

1752 • George Rogers Clark

1760? • Monk Estill

Anne McGinty

1750?–1815
- Started Kentucky's first clothing business
- Used local materials such as nettles to produce clothing and berries to color it

Jane Coomes

1750–1816
- Was Kentucky's first educator
- Established the first school in Kentucky at Fort Harrod in 1776
- Succeeded even though her school had little money and few supplies

George Nicholas

1742–1793
- One of Kentucky's most important pioneers
- Founded Fort Harrod, the first permanent European settlement in Kentucky, in 1775

1743–1799
- Served as an officer during the American Revolution
- Argued that Kentucky should separate from Virginia and become a new state
- Helped write Kentucky's first constitution

1790 | **1820** | **1850**

1794
1820
1793
1799
1815
1816
1818
1835

George Rogers Clark

Monk Estill

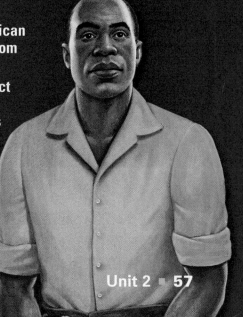

1752–1818
- Fought against the British during the American Revolution
- Helped defeat the British north of the Ohio River
- Defended settlers in Kentucky from the British and some Native Americans

1760?–1835
- Was the first enslaved African to gain freedom in Kentucky
- Helped protect Kentucky's early settlers
- Became a minister

MAINE
(part of MA)

Montreal

Lake Superior

Lake Michigan

Lake Huron

Lake Ontario

Lake Erie

NH

Portsmouth

MA

Boston

Providence

NY

CT

RI

New York City

PA

NJ

Philadelphia

ATLANTIC
OCEAN

Pittsburgh

DE
Annapolis
MD

Ohio River

Boonesborough
Harrod's Fort

KENTUCKY

VA

Williamsburg

New
Bern

NC

APPALACHIAN MOUNTAINS

Mississippi River

At The Same Time

Independence Hall, in Philadelphia

SC

NEW SPAIN

GA

Charles Town

Savannah

St. Augustine

N
W · E
S

New Orleans

San Antonio

Ohio River

Mississippi River

Tennessee River

0	150	300 Miles
0	150	300 Kilometers

Albers Equal-Area Projection

—— Major road

—— Native American trail

—— Pioneer trail

—— National border

—— State border

Boonesborough

Fort Harrod

Daniel Boone at the
Cumberland Gap

Ohio River

Salt River

Licking

Ohio River

Kentucky

Fort Harrod

Boonesborough

Danville

Logan's Station

Crab
Orchard

WARRIOR'S PATH

WILDERNESS TRAIL

Green River

River

Cumberland River

Cumberland Gap

Time

1600 — 1700 — 1800

1674
Gabriel Arthur travels from Virginia to Kentucky

1750
Dr. Thomas Walker finds the Cumberland Gap

1763
The Proclamation of 1763 is issued

WHAT TO KNOW
Why did the French and the British explore Kentucky?

VOCABULARY
colony p. 61
colonist p. 61
grant p. 63
gap p. 64
fort p. 65
ally p. 66
proclamation p. 67

PEOPLE
René-Robert Cavelier, Sieur de La Salle
Gabriel Arthur
Christopher Gist
Dr. Thomas Walker
John Howard
King George III

PLACES
Virginia
Appalachian Mountains
Cumberland Gap

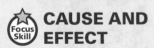

CAUSE AND EFFECT

Exploration of Kentucky

YOU ARE THERE

You are out of breath. It was a very long hike and a very steep climb. Finally, you are about to reach the top of a forested mountain in the Appalachians. It has taken hours to reach this point. You are tired. Your ears and nose are cold as the wind swirls around you. The top is just a few steps away. You wonder what you will see when you first glimpse the land that the Native Americans call Kentucky.

Why Explore Kentucky?

The first English settlers arrived in North America in the early 1600s. They sailed across the Atlantic Ocean and built settlements along the Atlantic coast. Settlements grew into colonies. A **colony** is a land ruled by a distant country. **Virginia** was one of the early English colonies in North America.

Looking Westward

By the late 1600s, some Virginia **colonists**, or people who lived in the colony, began to think about moving farther west. Native Americans called the land to the west Kentucky. No one is sure about the meaning of the word *Kentucky*, but some think it means "meadowland."

The colonists had different reasons for looking westward. Some wanted the adventure of exploring a new place. Others hoped to get rich by fur trapping or trading with Native Americans. Still others wanted to start farms by claiming land in Kentucky that no one owned. Later, many colonists did not like living under British laws. They hoped to find freedom in Kentucky.

READING CHECK ⏱ **CAUSE AND EFFECT**
Why did the colonists look westward?

> ⚡ **FAST FACT**
>
> No one knows exactly what Kentucky's name means. Some Native American meanings for the word *Kentucky* include "meadowland," "planted field," "land of tomorrow," and "red land."

❯ **GEOGRAPHY** The mountains that cover much of Kentucky made travel difficult for explorers. However, Kentucky's many streams and rivers helped with travel.

French Claims

English colonists were not the only Europeans interested in Kentucky. While the English were settling the Atlantic coast, the French were exploring territory farther inland. The French were the first Europeans to claim the territory of Kentucky.

In 1682, a French explorer named **René-Robert Cavelier, Sieur de La Salle**, claimed Kentucky and all of the Mississippi River valley for France.

Into the Wilderness

Kentucky was a wilderness. It had no roads or towns. Early explorers in the area traveled on foot and on horseback, often using trails made by the Native Americans. Sometimes they traveled in canoes copied from those of the Native Americans. The explorers carried their supplies with them and hunted for food. Mountains and forests made travel slow and difficult.

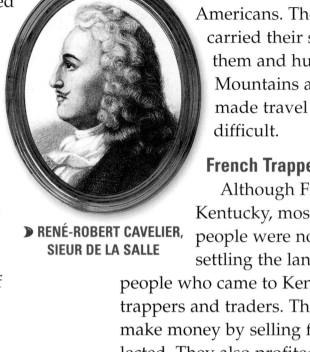

➤ RENÉ-ROBERT CAVELIER, SIEUR DE LA SALLE

French Trappers and Traders

Although France claimed Kentucky, most of the French people were not interested in settling the land. The French people who came to Kentucky were trappers and traders. Their goal was to make money by selling furs they collected. They also profited by trading with the Native Americans.

READING CHECK ⏀ **CAUSE AND EFFECT**
Why did the French not settle in Kentucky?

➤ **FRENCH TRAPPERS AND TRADERS** sometimes traveled with Native Americans on Kentucky's waterways.

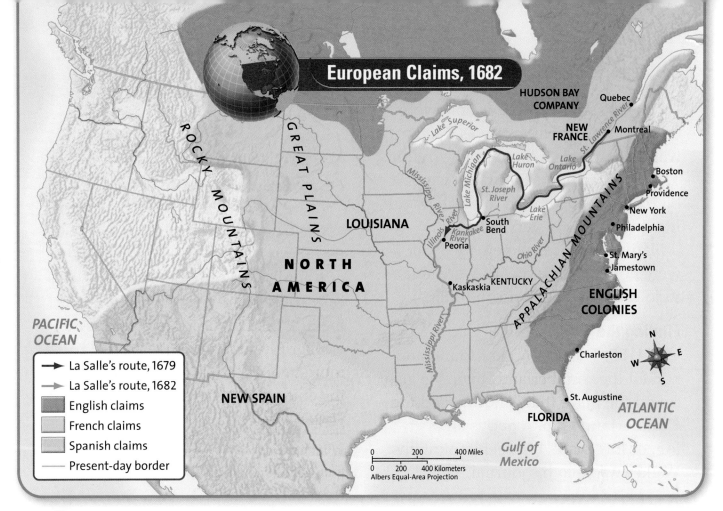

European Claims, 1682

HUDSON BAY COMPANY

Quebec

NEW FRANCE · Montreal

GREAT PLAINS

ROCKY MOUNTAINS

Lake Superior

St. Lawrence River

Lake Huron

Lake Ontario

Lake Erie

Lake Michigan

Mississippi River

St. Joseph River

Kankakee River

Illinois River

South Bend

Peoria

Ohio River

Boston

Providence

New York

Philadelphia

St. Mary's

Jamestown

APPALACHIAN MOUNTAINS

LOUISIANA

NORTH AMERICA

Kaskaskia

KENTUCKY

ENGLISH COLONIES

PACIFIC OCEAN

Charleston

NEW SPAIN

Mississippi River

St. Augustine

FLORIDA

ATLANTIC OCEAN

Gulf of Mexico

→ La Salle's route, 1679
→ La Salle's route, 1682
■ English claims
■ French claims
■ Spanish claims
— Present-day border

0   200   400 Miles
0   200   400 Kilometers
Albers Equal-Area Projection

 MAP SKILL **REGIONS** By 1682, the English, the French, and the Spanish had claimed lands in North America. In which year did La Salle travel near Kentucky?

British Explorers

Many Virginia colonists saw Kentucky as a land of opportunity. Exploring it was not easy, however.

The First Explorers

In 1674, **Gabriel Arthur** was one of the first Virginians to travel to Kentucky. Friendly Native Americans helped him. He returned to Virginia, telling stories of his adventures. He said that Kentucky would be a good place to live in.

In 1750, the Ohio Land Company received from the government a land grant of 200,000 acres, part of which was in Kentucky. A **grant** is an official document that gives permission for something. **Christopher Gist** explored the land for the company. He cleared a trail and scouted for resources.

At about the same time, **Dr. Thomas Walker** explored a land grant given to the Loyal Land Company. This grant covered 800,000 acres in Virginia and southeastern Kentucky. High mountains separated Kentucky from Virginia. They kept most people from entering Kentucky from the east.

READING CHECK ☼ **CAUSE AND EFFECT**
How did Gabriel Arthur encourage people to explore Kentucky?

A Breakthrough

One reason that more people were not coming to Kentucky was that it was so hard to get there from Virginia. The **Appalachian Mountains** were high and steep enough to make traveling through them very difficult.

Native Americans knew the land well, however. Europeans were able to follow Native American trails.

Finding the Gap

In 1750, Thomas Walker found and named the Cumberland River. He also found the place that is now called the **Cumberland Gap**. A **gap** is an opening, or low place, between mountains. Walker wrote in his journal,

> **❝**This gap may be seen at a considerable [long] distance, and there is no other, that I know of, except one about two miles to the north of it, which does not appear to be so low. . . . **❞**

The Cumberland Gap was important to the exploration and settlement of Kentucky. It provided the first easy route from Virginia to Kentucky, making the trip faster and safer. After Walker found the Cumberland Gap, more people came to Kentucky from the colonies.

READING CHECK ⟳**CAUSE AND EFFECT**
What physical feature prevented many people from settling Kentucky?

❯ **THE CUMBERLAND GAP** was a passageway through the Appalachian Mountains, which had kept early settlers from entering eastern Kentucky.

▶ **BRITISH FORTS** This photograph shows a re-creation of Fort Necessity in western Pennsylvania. Fort Necessity was one of the forts that the British built to help protect their western lands from the French.

Ready for a Fight

British explorers, hunters, and traders ignored France's claim to own Kentucky. For a long time, the French also ignored British activities in Kentucky. However, when more and more British people arrived through the Cumberland Gap, the French decided to take action. They did not want to share Kentucky's wealth with the British.

Defending Their Claims

In 1742, the French arrested **John Howard**, a British explorer of Kentucky, and sent him to France to be put on trial. This showed that they saw the British presence as illegal.

At about the same time, the French began to build forts on land they claimed. A **fort** is a strong building or area that can be defended against enemy attacks. The king of France sent soldiers to live in the forts. These soldiers tried to keep the British away from the land that French traders and trappers used.

British leaders did not like having French forts so near to lands they wanted to settle. The British said Kentucky was their land. The British also began to build forts to defend their western lands. Trouble was ahead for Kentucky.

READING CHECK ⚙ **CAUSE AND EFFECT**
Why did the British build forts?

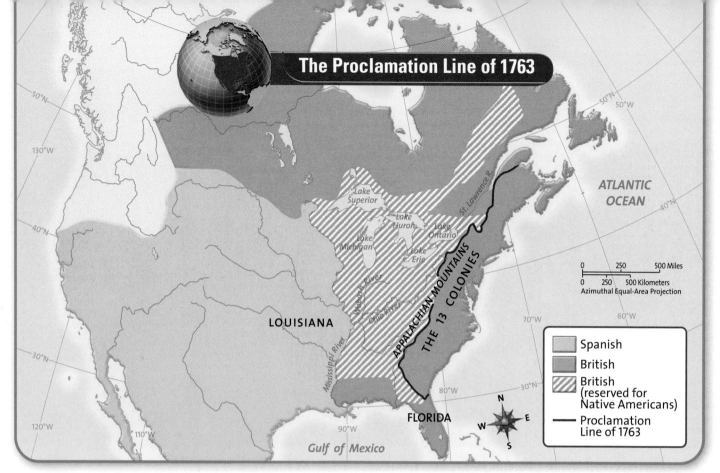

The Proclamation Line of 1763

ATLANTIC OCEAN

Lake Superior
Lake Huron
Lake Michigan
Lake Ontario
Lake Erie
St. Lawrence R.
APPALACHIAN MOUNTAINS
THE 13 COLONIES
Wabash River
Ohio River
Mississippi River

LOUISIANA

FLORIDA

Gulf of Mexico

0   250   500 Miles
0   250   500 Kilometers
Azimuthal Equal-Area Projection

Spanish
British
British (reserved for Native Americans)
Proclamation Line of 1763

N E S W

MAP SKILL HUMAN-ENVIRONMENT INTERACTIONS The Proclamation Line of 1763 marked the place farthest west where English colonists could settle. What physical feature marked the Proclamation Line?

War Over Land

The British and the French both claimed land west of the 13 colonies. This land included Kentucky. In 1754, these competing claims led to war.

The French and Indian War

This war is known as the French and Indian War. Many Native American groups fought as allies of the French. An **ally** is a partner in war. Other Native American groups fought as allies of the British.

Some Native Americans fought for the French because they traded with them. Also, the French did not build settlements on their land. The French

and their Native American allies wanted to keep British settlers out of Kentucky and the rest of the western lands.

The biggest battles of the French and Indian War took place to the north of Kentucky. Still, Kentucky was a dangerous place during the war. The French gave guns to Native Americans and encouraged them to attack settlers.

Kentucky's future was at stake. Would the region belong to the French or the British?

In 1763, Britain won the war. France lost most of its land in North America, including Kentucky.

READING CHECK ⟳ CAUSE AND EFFECT
What caused the French and Indian War?

Order from the King

After the French and Indian War, France gave Britain most of the land it claimed in North America. The Native Americans were angry because they lived on much of this land. From their point of view, France was giving Britain their land. Many prepared to start fighting again.

The Proclamation of 1763

To prevent war, Britain's **King George III** issued the Proclamation of 1763. A **proclamation** is an order from a country's leader to its citizens. He said that all land west of the Appalachian Mountains was for the Native Americans. British colonists could not explore, hunt on, or settle on that land. Settlers who lived there were ordered to leave.

READING CHECK ⓒ**CAUSE AND EFFECT**
What was the Proclamation of 1763?

❭ **KING GEORGE III (above) issued the Proclamation of 1763 (right).**

Summary

French trappers and traders explored Kentucky. British explorers from Virginia also began to travel to Kentucky. The British and the French fought in the French and Indian War. In 1763, the British won, but their king made traveling to Kentucky illegal for them.

REVIEW

1. **WHAT TO KNOW** Why did the French and the British explore Kentucky?

2. **VOCABULARY** Use the words **gap** and **grant** in a sentence about the exploration of Kentucky.

3. **HISTORY** Who found the Cumberland Gap? Why was this discovery important?

4. **CRITICAL THINKING** How did disagreements over land use lead to conflict in the western lands?

5. ✎ **WRITE A PERSUASIVE LETTER** Imagine that you want to move to Kentucky, but you have just learned about the Proclamation of 1763. Write a letter to the king, explaining why moving to Kentucky should be allowed.

6. ⭐(Focus Skill) **CAUSE AND EFFECT** On a separate sheet of paper, copy and complete the graphic organizer below.

Cause	Effect
More and more British settlers arrived in Kentucky.	

Use an Elevation Map

Why It Matters Elevation (eh•luh•VAY•shuhn) is the height of the land above sea level. An elevation map can tell you how high or how low different areas of Kentucky are.

❱ LEARN

The present-day map on page 69 uses colors to show a range of elevations. This means that each color stands for an area's highest and lowest elevations, as well as all the elevations in between.

The map also uses shading to show **relief**, or differences in elevation. Dark shading shows steep rises and drops in elevation. Light shading shows gentle rises and drops. These are the same rises and drops in elevation that early explorers encountered.

❱ PRACTICE

Use the map to answer these questions.

1 Which part of Kentucky has high elevations?

2 What is the elevation around Louisville? Is the land there higher or lower than the land around Lexington?

3 Where is Kentucky's lowest elevation?

❱ **THE CUMBERLAND GAP** was a passageway through the mountains that helped promote the settlement of Kentucky.

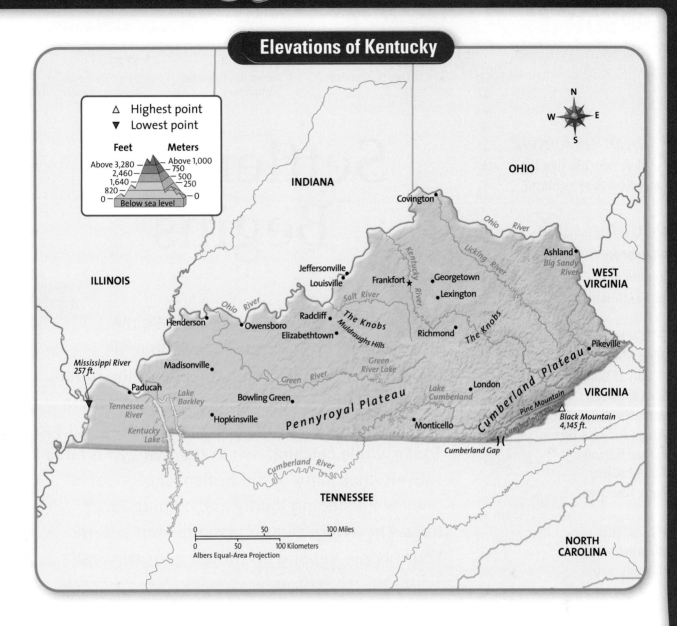

Elevations of Kentucky

△ Highest point
▼ Lowest point

Feet   Meters
Above 3,280 — Above 1,000
        — 750
2,460 — 500
1,640 — 250
820 —
0 — Below sea level — 0

APPLY

Imagine that you are an early explorer of Kentucky. Write a journal entry about the different elevations you cross as you travel from the eastern end of Kentucky to the western end. Describe the challenges of traveling through the mountains.

Map and Globe Skills

Time

1600	1700	1800

1774
Lord Dunmore's War

1775
James Harrod settles
Harrodsburg

1775
Daniel Boone begins
building Boonesborough

WHAT TO KNOW
What was life like for early Kentucky settlers?

VOCABULARY
pioneer p. 72
frontier p. 72
self-sufficient p. 76

PEOPLE
John Murray,
   Earl of Dunmore
Daniel Boone
John Finley
Judge Richard Henderson
James Harrod
Ann McGinty
Jane Coomes

PLACES
Boonesborough
Harrodsburg

CAUSE AND EFFECT

Settlement Begins

YOU ARE THERE Your father is upset. In 1763, the British king had declared that his people would remain on their side of the mountains. Everything on this side was to remain in the hands of your people and neighboring tribes. Today, while catching fish in the river, your father saw another party of the British king's people. They were singing loudly and cutting down trees. They were clearing land to start a farm. Your people depend on this land for survival!

▶ **SETTLERS** began to clear land and build homes on Native American hunting grounds.

▶ **THE OHIO RIVER VALLEY** Cornstalk (left) led the Shawnee against Lord Dunmore (right) and his soldiers in the fight to control the Ohio River valley.

Native Americans Fight On

Many British colonists ignored the Proclamation of 1763 and continued to settle west of the Appalachians. Some Native American groups fought to force settlers off their hunting lands.

Lord Dunmore's War

In 1774, fighting broke out between British colonists north of the Ohio River and the Shawnee. The side that won would control the Ohio River valley. From there, they could control Kentucky.

The British governor of Virginia, **John Murray, Earl of Dunmore**, had to protect the colonists. He also knew how important it was to control the Ohio River valley. In May, he set out with more than 1,000 soldiers and traveled to the area north of the Ohio River. In October, after a terrible battle that lasted for a whole day, the Shawnee and their allies were defeated.

To end the war, the British and the Native Americans signed the Treaty of Camp Charlotte. In this treaty, settlers gained the right to hunt in Kentucky and to travel on the Ohio River.

Even though the war did not take place in Kentucky, it was very important for Kentucky's history. It helped make Kentucky a safer place to settle.

READING CHECK ⏰**CAUSE AND EFFECT**
What was one effect of Lord Dunmore's War?

A Promising Land

Daniel Boone was one of the most important pioneers in Kentucky. A **pioneer** is a person who first settles a new place. Boone became famous for his courage and skill in exploring and settling the American **frontier**, or land that lies beyond settled areas.

Early Days

Daniel Boone was born in 1734 in Pennsylvania. His parents later moved the family to North Carolina. During the French and Indian War, Boone met **John Finley**. Finley was a fur trader who had traveled in Kentucky. Finley told Boone stories about the fertile land and wild game in Kentucky.

Attempts to Settle

Boone first tried to start a Kentucky settlement in 1773. He gathered a group of people who planned to settle with him. Native Americans attacked Boone's group along the way. Some of the settlers were killed, including Boone's oldest son, James. In spite of this, Boone wanted to keep going. The others refused, however, and the group went back to Virginia.

Two years later, Boone headed for Kentucky again. This time, **Judge Richard Henderson** hired Boone

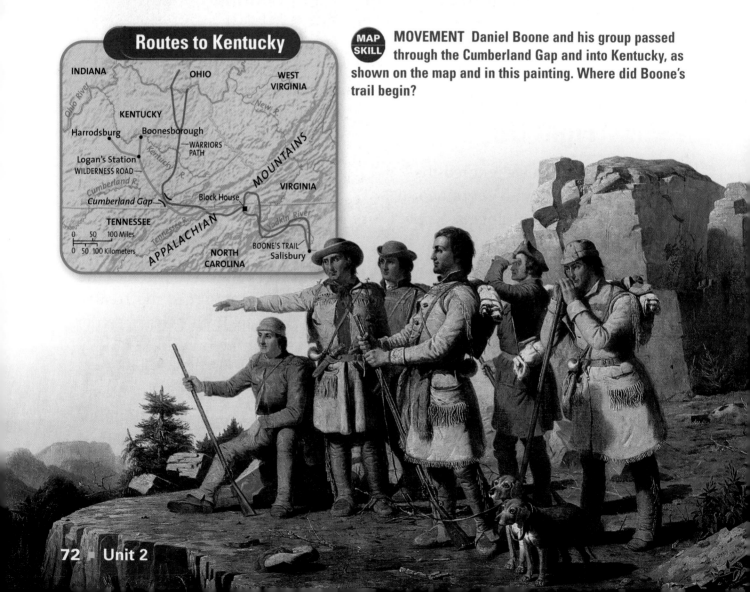

Routes to Kentucky

INDIANA
OHIO
WEST VIRGINIA
Ohio River
New R.
KENTUCKY
Harrodsburg
Boonesborough
WARRIORS PATH
Logan's Station
WILDERNESS ROAD
Kentucky R.
Cumberland R.
APPALACHIAN MOUNTAINS
VIRGINIA
Cumberland Gap
Block House
Yadkin River
TENNESSEE
0   50   100 Miles
0   50 100 Kilometers
Tennessee R.
BOONE'S TRAIL
Salisbury
NORTH CAROLINA

MAP SKILL **MOVEMENT** Daniel Boone and his group passed through the Cumberland Gap and into Kentucky, as shown on the map and in this painting. Where did Boone's trail begin?

Jemima Boone

Jemima Boone was the daughter of Daniel and Rebecca Boone. She traveled to Kentucky with her parents in 1775.

On July 14, 1776, Jemima, age 13, and two friends were canoeing on the Kentucky River. Shawnee warriors kidnapped the girls. As the Shawnee led the girls back to their camp, Jemima tore off small pieces of her dress and left them behind. She knew that her father could use these clues to find her. He did. He and some other men from Boonesborough found the girls and rescued them.

Make It Relevant How did Jemima Boone show courage?

to start a settlement. Henderson had bought land from the Cherokee. Henderson knew that Boone had the skills to build a town in the wilderness.

Thirty-five men went with Boone to Kentucky in 1775. They passed through the rough mountain terrain and cut a trail through the forest. Boone also brought most of his family with him.

The settlers traveled through the Cumberland Gap. This group, too, was attacked by Native Americans. Unlike the earlier group, they kept going.

Boonesborough

Boone started the settlement on the south bank of the Kentucky River. He began by building a road and a fort. Things did not always go well for Boone and the settlers with him. Building the road took longer than expected. Money to pay the workers ran out. In the beginning, food was scarce. Gradually, however, the settlement became a success.

Henderson was very pleased with Boone's work. He named the settlement **Boonesborough** and gave Boone 5,000 acres of land.

Boonesborough was a busy village for decades. Today, no one lives in Boonesborough. The site is Fort Boonesborough State Park. The fort has been rebuilt so that visitors can experience what life on the frontier was like.

READING CHECK ☼ **CAUSE AND EFFECT**

Why did Boone become interested in exploring and settling Kentucky?

Foothold in Kentucky

James Harrod was another important pioneer. He had much in common with Daniel Boone. Both men were from Pennsylvania. Harrod and Boone began their settlements at about the same time, and both villages were near the Kentucky River.

Forced to Leave

In 1774, Harrod and 31 other men left Pennsylvania and headed for Kentucky. They paddled canoes up the Kentucky River. In June, the group reached the site where they wanted to settle. They built cabins and began to clear land so they could farm. However, attacks by Native Americans forced the settlers to leave Harrod's Town behind.

Harrodsburg

A year later, Harrod returned to the site with about 50 other settlers. Together, they built a fort. The fort allowed them to defend themselves against attacks by Native Americans. The group renamed the settlement **Harrodsburg**.

Harrodsburg became the first permanent European settlement in Kentucky. In fact, Harrodsburg was the site of many "firsts" in Kentucky

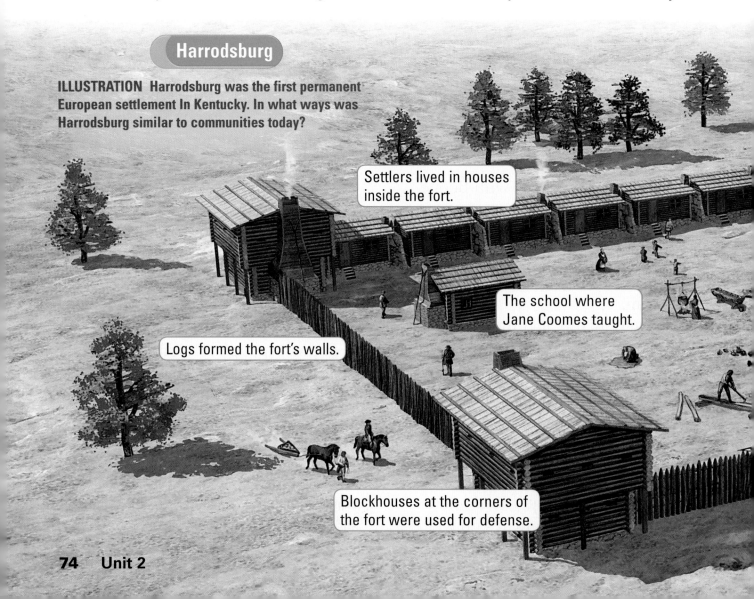

Harrodsburg

ILLUSTRATION Harrodsburg was the first permanent European settlement In Kentucky. In what ways was Harrodsburg similar to communities today?

Settlers lived in houses inside the fort.

The school where Jane Coomes taught.

Logs formed the fort's walls.

Blockhouses at the corners of the fort were used for defense.

history. Settlers there made the first plow that was used in the region.

When **Ann McGinty** arrived in Harrodsburg, she brought with her the first spinning wheel ever used in Kentucky. A spinning wheel is a tool used to make thread for clothing.

Harrodsburg was also the site of Kentucky's first school. The teacher was **Jane Coomes**, who came to the village from Maryland. Students at the school learned reading and arithmetic. They did not have books like the ones students use today. Instead, they had hornbooks. A hornbook was a piece of wood shaped like a paddle and covered with a sheet of horn. Horn is a material made from the horns of animals. The alphabet and Christian prayers were written or printed on the hornbook.

At Harrodsburg, James Harrod had a large, successful farm. Eventually, he owned thousands of acres of land in different parts of Kentucky.

Today, about 8,000 people live in Harrodsburg. Visitors can tour the rebuilt Fort Harrod and see how people lived in the early settlement.

READING CHECK **MAIN IDEA AND DETAILS**
What are some of the Kentucky "firsts" that Harrodsburg is known for?

Corral for livestock

Gates could be closed in case of an attack

A creek provided water.

Pioneer Life

In Kentucky, farmland and wild game were plentiful. Settlers began moving to Kentucky in larger and larger numbers. They moved to Kentucky knowing that they would have to work hard to survive.

Rugged Settlers

The people who settled Kentucky were pioneers. Pioneers were largely self-sufficient. **Self-sufficient** means being able to do everything for oneself, with no help from others.

Providing for one's own needs was important on the frontier. Settlers on the frontier lived far from towns, stores, and doctors. The nearest neighbors might live miles away.

Most pioneer cabins had just one room. A fireplace served as both heater and stove for cooking. Settlers carried water from streams for cooking and washing. They made soap from animal fat. Farmers used simple tools that they made and repaired themselves. They also made their own furniture, toys, dishes, and clothing.

❯ PIONEERS These reenactors (next page) show how hard Kentucky pioneers worked to be self-sufficient. Pioneers made many of the things they needed, and they traded for things they could not make themselves.

Butter press

Iron

Serving platter with silverware

Working Together

Even self-sufficient settlers needed help at times. Often families helped each other build cabins. Settlers worked together to cut down trees and shape them into logs. Then they fitted the logs together to form strong walls.

Pioneers traded with each other to get things they could not make themselves. For example, a man who specialized in making horseshoes might trade them for clothing made by a woman who specialized in sewing. Most pioneers used very little money.

READING CHECK ⟳ **CAUSE AND EFFECT**
Why did settlers on the frontier have to be self-sufficient?

Summary

Many colonists ignored the Proclamation of 1763 and continued to settle in Kentucky. Daniel Boone and James Harrod started early settlements there. Pioneers had to be nearly self-sufficient to survive.

REVIEW

1. **WHAT TO KNOW** What was life like for early Kentucky settlers?

2. **VOCABULARY** Use the term **pioneer** to write a sentence about the **frontier**.

3. **HISTORY** Who started the first permanent European settlement in Kentucky?

4. **CRITICAL THINKING** Why do you think both Harrodsburg and Boonesborough were built near the Kentucky River?

5. ✏ **WRITE A SCENE FOR A PLAY** With a partner, write a short scene for a play about pioneers in Kentucky. Write lines for two characters.

6. **Focus Skill** **CAUSE AND EFFECT** On a separate sheet of paper, copy and complete the graphic organizer below.

Cause	Effect
Pioneers needed some things they could not make themselves.	

FIELD TRIP

READ ABOUT

FORT BOONESBOROUGH STATE PARK

Today, visitors can come to the very spot where Daniel Boone built his fort. Although the original is gone, an authentic reconstruction shows visitors what it looked like. It was built to show what life was like for pioneers in the late 1700s.

Visitors can watch blacksmiths, weavers, and other craftworkers. There is also a museum that displays numerous pioneer artifacts—the things people needed to survive in Kentucky's wilderness. Fort Boonesborough State Park offers visitors a glimpse into the past.

FIND

KENTUCKY

Fort Boonesborough State Park

RE-ENACTORS show what life was like at Boonesborough.

STITCHING

MAKING CANDLES

RECREATING THE SIEGE OF
BOONESBOROUGH

A BLACKSMITH

THE ART OF QUILTING

A VIRTUAL TOUR

GO ONLINE For more resources go to
www.harcourtschool.com/ss1

Pioneer Artifacts

Background In the late 1700s, more and more people began to pour into the western frontier—including Kentucky. They wanted to begin new lives on new land of their own. They left behind many artifacts that give us clues about how the pioneers lived.

DBQ Document-Based Question Study these primary sources and answer the questions.

LEATHER POUCH

This pouch may have belonged to Daniel Boone

DBQ ❶ What items might this pouch have contained?

POWDER HORN

This horn was used to store gunpowder.

DBQ ❷ Why might a pioneer need to have gunpowder with him or her?

KETTLE

A kettle could be used to boil water and to cook food.

DBQ ❸ How would metal cookware improve life on the frontier?

AXE

An axe was needed to cut down trees and to shape logs for building houses and forts.

DBQ ❹ Why might pioneers have preferred simple tools?

SPINNING WHEEL

This spinning wheel made fabric for clothing and other uses.

DBQ ❺ Why might pioneers have wanted to be able to make their own clothing?

WRITE ABOUT IT

What do these artifacts tell you about life on the Kentucky frontier? Write a paragraph to describe frontier life.

GO ONLINE For more resources, go to www.harcourtschool.com/ss1

Time

1600   1700   1800

1775
The American
Revolution begins

1782
The Battle of Blue Licks

1783
A peace treaty
ends the American
Revolution

WHAT TO KNOW
How did the American
Revolution affect
Kentucky?

VOCABULARY
tax p. 83
independence p. 83
revolution p. 83
station p. 84
militia p. 85

PEOPLE
Daniel Boone
Simon Kenton
George Rogers Clark
Captain Henry Hamilton
Captain James Estill
Monk Estill

PLACES
Logan's Station
Boonesborough
Harrodsburg
Kaskaskia
Vincennes
Northwest Territory
Yorktown, Virginia

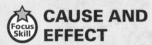

CAUSE AND EFFECT

The American Revolution

YOU ARE THERE

The year is 1777, and the 13 colonies are
at war with Britain. The British have been
encouraging their Native American allies to attack
settlements in Kentucky.

You and your family are huddled inside a cabin
at **Logan's Station**. All the settlers in the area
fled to the station when word came that a group
of Native Americans was about to attack.

Warriors are now camped outside the station.
They know that sooner or later someone must
come out to get food and water. You are very
hungry, yet you hope no one has to go outside
in search of food.

A War for Freedom

While more and more people were settling Kentucky, a war began in the 13 colonies. Kentucky now belonged to Virginia. It had been declared a part of Virginia's Fincastle County in 1772.

Anger Over Taxes

For years, the British rulers had been forcing colonists to pay more and more taxes without giving them representation in the British government. A **tax** is money that a government collects to pay for the services it provides. The heavy taxes and lack of representation angered colonists. The taxes no longer seemed necessary, since the war with France was over. Finally, in 1775, anger turned to war. Fights broke out between colonists and British soldiers.

In 1776, the colonies declared their independence from Britain. **Independence** is the freedom to govern on one's own. Britain fought to keep the colonies under its rule.

Native Americans Join the Fight

The colonists' war for independence is called the American Revolution, or the Revolutionary War. A **revolution** is a sudden, great change, such as the overthrow of a government.

The main battles of the American Revolution took place east of Kentucky. Few British soldiers were in Kentucky. However, settlers in Kentucky did not escape the war. As the French had done earlier, the British encouraged Native Americans to fight the settlers.

READING CHECK ↻ **CAUSE AND EFFECT**
What caused the American Revolution?

❯ **THE BATTLE OF BUNKER HILL** in Massachusetts was one of the early battles of the American Revolution.

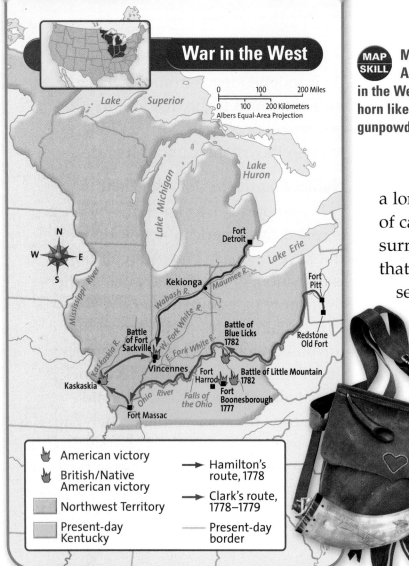

War in the West

MAP SKILL **MOVEMENT** This map shows some of the American Revolution battles that took place in the West. Many soldiers carried a pouch and a horn like these (below), which held musket balls and gunpowder. Which battles took place in Kentucky?

Lake Superior

Lake Michigan

Lake Huron

Lake Erie

Fort Detroit

Kekionga

Maumee R.

Wabash R.

Fort Pitt

N. Fork White R.

E. Fork White R.

Battle of Blue Licks 1782

Redstone Old Fort

Battle of Fort Sackville

Vincennes

Fort Harrod

Battle of Little Mountain 1782

Kaskaskia R.

Mississippi River

Kaskaskia

Ohio River

Falls of the Ohio

Fort Boonesborough 1777

Fort Massac

American victory
British/Native American victory
Northwest Territory
Present-day Kentucky

Hamilton's route, 1778
Clark's route, 1778–1779
Present-day border

a long, fenced-in cabin to a group of cabins with a stockade fence surrounding them. When word came that an attack was expected, the settlers ran to the forts or stations for protection.

Native American fighters often camped outside the forts. They hoped the settlers would run out of food and water and be forced to come out.

In April 1777, more than 400 Shawnee attacked the fort at Boonesborough. **Daniel Boone** and the other settlers outlasted the attackers.

Simon Kenton of Boonesborough is remembered for his courage during the war. He sneaked into and out of the fort to hunt for food and carried messages between groups of settlers. He may even have saved Daniel Boone's life. When Boone was shot in the ankle during the fighting, he fell and was almost unconscious. Kenton picked him up and carried him back to safety in the fort.

The War in Kentucky

As fighting between Kentucky settlers and some Native American groups increased, many pioneers fled to the East. The number of settlers in Kentucky dropped from more than 10,000 to fewer than 300.

Safety at Forts and Stations

The few remaining settlers stayed near the forts at **Boonesborough** and **Harrodsburg** and at nearby stations. A **station** was a fortified outpost that was smaller than a fort. The size of a station ranged from

READING CHECK ☌ **CAUSE AND EFFECT**
Why did the number of settlers in Kentucky drop during the war?

George Rogers Clark

George Rogers Clark was an important leader in Kentucky during the American Revolution. He helped protect the Kentucky settlers both on the battlefield and off.

Defending Kentucky

In 1776, Clark worked to make Kentucky a separate county of Virginia. He believed that Kentucky settlers could better defend themselves if Kentucky had its own county government. Virginia leaders made the decision on December 31. Clark was given 500 pounds of gunpowder to help defend the new Virginia county.

Clark also led the Kentucky militia. A **militia** is a volunteer army. Daniel Boone and James Harrod joined the Kentucky militia, which worked to protect settlers.

▶ GEORGE ROGERS CLARK

In 1778, Clark and his militia made a surprise attack on two British forts. The Kentuckians captured both **Kaskaskia** and **Vincennes** in the neighboring **Northwest Territory**. This land later became the states of Illinois, Indiana, Ohio, Wisconsin, Michigan, and part of Minnesota.

Fighting Back

Later that year, a British soldier, **Captain Henry Hamilton**, recaptured Vincennes. Clark did not accept defeat at Hamilton's hands. In January 1779, Clark again captured Vincennes and the British soldiers there, including Hamilton.

READING CHECK ⟳ **CAUSE AND EFFECT Why did Kentucky become a Virginia county?**

▶ **MARCHING** General George Rogers Clark led his troops through many miles of rough terrain.

Fighting Continues

The American colonies won the war in 1781. British forces surrendered to the Americans at **Yorktown**, **Virginia**. However, fighting was not yet over in Kentucky and other parts of the west. British soldiers encouraged their Native American allies to continue to fight against settlers.

The Battle of Little Mountain

On March 19, 1782, **Captain James Estill** led about 25 Kentucky settlers against a group of Wyandot near what is today Mount Sterling, in Montgomery County. James Estill was killed in the fighting, and 13 other settlers were killed or seriously wounded. Estill's enslaved African servant **Monk Estill** survived and carried an injured settler nearly 25 miles to safety.

The Battle of Blue Licks

Even though the British had already surrendered at Yorktown, the largest Revolutionary War battle in Kentucky took place after most of the fighting had stopped.

On August 19, 1782, about 200 Kentucky militiamen were riding in pursuit of a raiding party that had attacked Bryan's Station near Lexington. Daniel Boone and his son Israel were part of the group. Near the Licking River, in what is now Robertson County, the militiamen

> **THE BATTLE OF BLUE LICKS** was the largest Revolutionary War battle in Kentucky. Today, a monument (left) honors those who died.

ANDREW KNEZ JR.

spotted the large group of Native Americans with a few British soldiers.

Boone told the Kentucky soldiers not to attack, because they were greatly outnumbered. The soldiers did not listen to Boone. They attacked anyway. The battle was very short but bloody. In the end, 60 Kentuckians were killed, including Israel Boone. The Battle of Blue Licks is known today as one of the worst American military disasters that took place on the Kentucky frontier.

The American Revolution Ends

The Battle of Blue Licks was the last big battle between settlers and Native Americans in Kentucky. In 1783, the new United States of America signed a peace treaty with Britain. The British gave up their claims to the colonies. The American Revolution finally ended in Kentucky. Settlers were now free from British control.

READING CHECK **SUMMARIZE**
What happened in Kentucky after the British surrender at Yorktown?

▶ **THE TREATY OF PARIS** In 1783, American leaders made a peace agreement with the British and signed the Treaty of Paris (above right).

Summary

In 1775, the American colonies began a war for independence from Britain. British soldiers stationed at forts north of Kentucky encouraged Native Americans to attack settlers. Kentucky became a county of Virginia and formed a militia. The colonists won the American Revolution. Fighting ended with a peace treaty in 1783.

REVIEW

1. WHAT TO KNOW How did the American Revolution affect Kentucky?

2. VOCABULARY Use the word **independence** to help explain what a **revolution** is.

3. HISTORY Which Revolutionary War battles took place in Kentucky?

4. CRITICAL THINKING Why do you think fighting continued in Kentucky after British forces had already surrendered at Yorktown?

5. ✎ **WRITE A POEM** Write a poem about the American Revolution in Kentucky. Your poem does not have to rhyme, but it should have at least 8 lines.

6. (Focus Skill) **CAUSE AND EFFECT** On a separate sheet of paper, copy and complete the graphic organizer below.

Cause	Effect
	Many settlers fled Kentucky.

Biographies

Trustworthiness
Respect
Responsibility
Fairness
Caring
Patriotism

American Revolution Heroes

During the American Revolution, Kentuckians were called to battle. Not only did they fight for their homes, but they fought for the future of our whole nation. Suffering great hardships, Kentuckians supported independence from Britain.

Daniel Boone is remembered as one of Kentucky's great explorers. His Quaker parents lived in Pennsylvania, but he decided early in life that he wanted to live on the frontier. As soon as he was old enough, Daniel Boone began to go on hunting trips through the Cumberland Gap and into Kentucky.

Boone was often called on to fight against the British and the Native Americans. However, he much preferred exploring the land in peace. Because he knew the land, he was able to set up a route that settlers could take to make Kentucky their home.

Daniel Boone

1734–1820
Character Trait: Patriotism

Jane Coomes

1750–1816

Character Trait: Caring

Jane Coomes was Kentucky's first educator. She started the first school in Kentucky in 1776. It was at Fort Harrod. At the time, the people of Fort Harrod were under threat from the British and some Native American groups. Because of this, Coomes could not get many things to use at her school. For example, books were hard to get. Instead, Coomes and her students used hornbooks. The writing on them was not in ink. Coomes used charcoal and berry juice instead. Even with such simple things, Jane Coomes was able to teach the children of Kentucky.

Monk Estill was the first enslaved African to gain freedom in Kentucky. He came to Kentucky in the 1770s. His first job was tending an apple orchard in Boonesborough. In a battle against a group of Native Americans in 1782, Estill's owner was killed. Estill helped another settler who was wounded in the battle. He carried the settler to safety over a distance of 25 miles! He helped the settlers even more by making gunpowder. For his bravery and hard work, Estill was given his freedom. He went on to become a minister and died in Shelbyville in 1835.

Monk Estill

About 1760–1835

Character Trait: Trustworthiness

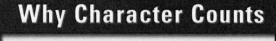

Why Character Counts

1. How did Daniel Boone show patriotism?

2. In what way did Jane Coomes show caring?

3. How did Monk Estill prove his trustworthiness?

GO ONLINE

For more resources, go to
www.harcourtschool.com/ss1

Time

1600	1700	1800

1784
Kentucky leaders
meet at Danville

1792
Kentucky becomes
a state

1799
Leaders write Kentucky's
second constitution

 WHAT TO KNOW
When and how did
Kentucky become a state?

VOCABULARY

census p. 91
boundary p. 92
constitution p. 93
democracy p. 94

PEOPLE

Francis Asbury
Colonel Benjamin Logan
George Nicholas
Isaac Shelby

PLACES

Danville
Frankfort

 **CAUSE AND EFFECT**

Statehood

YOU ARE THERE Your legs dangle off the boat, and you close your eyes. The sun warms your face and shines through the trees surrounding the river. The water is cool as it gushes between your toes. You hear the rhythmic *whoosh* of the huge oars lifting out of the water with every stroke.

Your family is moving to Kentucky. This is your last chance to rest before it's time to unload your flatboat and start a brand-new life.

Settlers Return

After the American Revolution, Kentucky was a safer place. Many people who had fled during the war returned. Many new settlers came, too.

Counting Kentuckians

Some of the new settlers had been soldiers in the American Revolution. The Virginia government paid many of its soldiers with military land warrants, or grants of land, in Kentucky. So many new settlers arrived in Kentucky in 1784 that some historians think the population doubled that year!

Many farmers came to Kentucky in search of inexpensive land. **Francis Asbury**, a Methodist bishop, often saw them making their way to Kentucky on his many travels there. He wrote of seeing

> **66** men, women, and children . . . paddling bare-foot and bare-legged along, or labouring [struggling] up the rocky hills. **99**

Other farmers made their way to Kentucky in large covered wagons. A few arrived with large herds of horses and cattle to start their new farms.

In 1790, the United States government carried out its first census. A **census** is an official population count. It showed that more than 70,000 people lived in Kentucky.

READING CHECK Ŏ **CAUSE AND EFFECT**
Why did former soldiers move to Kentucky?

▶ **FLATBOATS** Some settlers traveled by flatboat into Kentucky. Flatboats are boats that have flat bottoms and square ends.

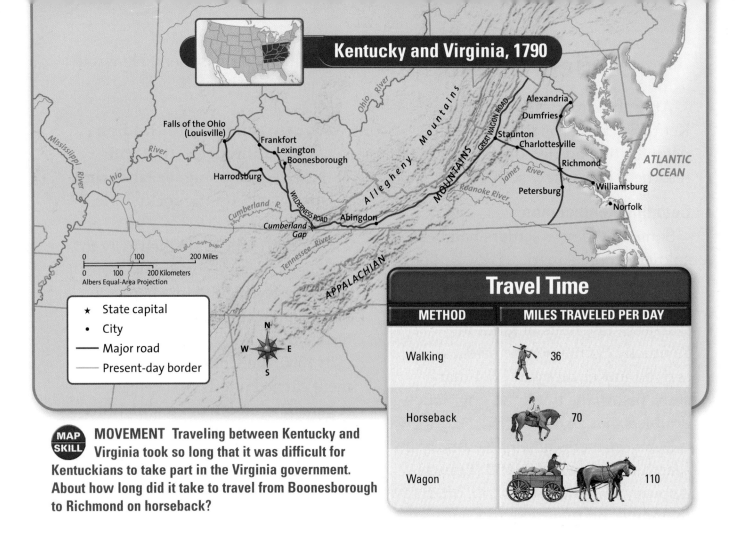

Kentucky and Virginia, 1790

ATLANTIC OCEAN

Alexandria
Dumfries
Staunton
Charlottesville
Richmond
Williamsburg
Petersburg
Norfolk

Falls of the Ohio (Louisville)
Frankfort
Lexington
Boonesborough
Harrodsburg
Abingdon
Cumberland Gap

Ohio River
Mississippi River
Cumberland R.
Tennessee River
Roanoke River
James River

Allegheny Mountains
APPALACHIAN MOUNTAINS
WILDERNESS ROAD
GREAT WAGON ROAD

0   100   200 Miles
0   100   200 Kilometers
Albers Equal-Area Projection

★ State capital
• City
— Major road
— Present-day border

Travel Time

METHOD		MILES TRAVELED PER DAY
Walking		36
Horseback		70
Wagon		110

MAP SKILL **MOVEMENT** Traveling between Kentucky and Virginia took so long that it was difficult for Kentuckians to take part in the Virginia government. About how long did it take to travel from Boonesborough to Richmond on horseback?

Reasons to Separate

In 1790, Kentucky was still part of Virginia, which was now a state. Many Kentuckians were ready for a change, however.

Complaints About Virginia

Kentuckians had some complaints about Virginia's government. One important complaint was about taxes. People in Kentucky had to pay taxes to Virginia. Yet Virginia provided few services to Kentuckians in return for their tax money.

Another complaint was about Virginia's laws dealing with Native Americans. Kentuckians had to get Virginia's permission before they could make any agreements with Native Americans inside and outside Kentucky's boundaries. A **boundary** is a line or point that indicates a limit. Under this law, Native Americans could attack Kentuckians and then flee across its boundaries for safety.

Kentuckians did have some voice in the Virginia government. However, their role was not strong enough to make a difference.

Many Kentuckians thought that Virginia's leaders were too far away to understand their problems. They wanted to separate from Virginia.

READING CHECK Ö**CAUSE AND EFFECT**
What complaints made Kentuckians want to separate from Virginia?

Choosing Statehood

Kentuckians did not all agree about how to solve their problems with Virginia. Kentucky leaders had to decide what to do.

Possible Solutions

In 1784, **Colonel Benjamin Logan** had called a meeting to talk about problems with Virginia. A group of leaders met in the town of **Danville**. Some leaders wanted to remain part of Virginia. They hoped the problems could be worked out.

Other leaders wanted Kentucky to be a country. They wanted Kentucky to declare its independence from the United States just as the colonies had declared their independence from Britain.

Still other leaders wanted Kentucky to become a state in the United States.

After holding ten conventions over an eight-year period, Kentuckians chose this solution.

Before being accepted as a state, Kentucky needed to write a constitution. A **constitution** is a plan of government.

George Nicholas, a lawyer, wrote much of Kentucky's constitution. For that reason, he has been called the "Father of the First Kentucky Constitution." Other leaders also contributed to the constitution. They finished writing the constitution in April 1792.

Kentucky became a state on June 1, 1792. It was the fifteenth state to join the United States. Kentucky was the first state west of the Appalachian Mountains.

READING CHECK ⭕ **CAUSE AND EFFECT**
Why did Kentucky leaders write a constitution?

> **THE DANVILLE COURTHOUSE,** where the first Kentucky Constitution was signed, is now a museum.

More Changes

Kentucky's leaders chose **Frankfort** as the state capital. They elected **Isaac Shelby** as their first governor. Still, the government was not yet final.

A New Constitution

Kentuckians soon began to see flaws in their state's constitution. Many people thought that the constitution gave too much power to the governor. For example, the governor had the power to appoint many state leaders. The people had no voice in the choices.

In 1799, state leaders wrote a new constitution that made changes to the old constitution. It gave the people of Kentucky more voice in their government. Under this constitution, voters elected more of the state's leaders.

The new constitution made Kentucky more of a democracy. A **democracy** is a form of government in which people rule by making decisions themselves, or by electing people to make decisions for them.

Kentucky's Model

Both Nicholas's constitution and the new constitution borrowed important ideas from the United States Constitution. One of these ideas was a government with three branches.

Like the United States government, Kentucky's government has a legislative branch, an executive branch,

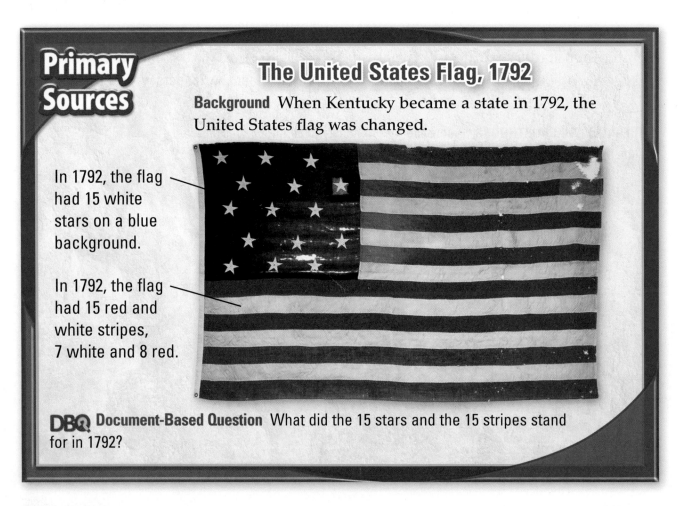

Primary Sources

The United States Flag, 1792

Background When Kentucky became a state in 1792, the United States flag was changed.

In 1792, the flag had 15 white stars on a blue background.

In 1792, the flag had 15 red and white stripes, 7 white and 8 red.

DBQ Document-Based Question What did the 15 stars and the 15 stripes stand for in 1792?

and a judicial branch. The legislative branch makes the laws. The executive branch carries out the laws. The judicial branch sees that the laws are carried out correctly and fairly.

Dividing the government into three branches keeps any one branch from having too much power. Each branch limits the power of the other two.

READING CHECK ⊙ **CAUSE AND EFFECT**
How did Kentucky's new constitution change Kentucky's government?

Summary

After the American Revolution, many people came to Kentucky. Kentucky became a state in 1792. Kentucky's leaders chose Frankfort to be the state capital and wrote a new constitution that gave the people more voice in their government.

❯ **ISAAC SHELBY** was Kentucky's first governor. He promised to defend Kentucky's new constitution (left).

REVIEW

1. **WHAT TO KNOW** When and how did Kentucky become a state?

2. **VOCABULARY** Write a sentence that uses the terms **constitution** and **democracy**.

3. **HISTORY** Who was Kentucky's first governor?

4. **CRITICAL THINKING** Do you think Kentucky's second constitution is better than the first one? Explain your answer.

5. ✎ **WRITE A PERSUASIVE LETTER** Imagine that you live in Kentucky in 1790. Write a letter to a friend about Kentucky's complaints about Virginia. Tell your friend what you think Kentucky should do.

6. ⭐ (Focus Skill) **CAUSE AND EFFECT** On a separate sheet of paper, copy and complete the graphic organizer below.

Cause		Effect
Kentuckians did not like paying taxes to Virginia.	▶	
Kentuckians did not like Virginia's laws about Native Americans.	▶	

Review and Test Prep

💡 THE BIG IDEA

Exploration and Settlement The exploration and settlement of Kentucky led to interactions between diverse peoples.

Reading Comprehension and Vocabulary

Europeans Settle Kentucky

In the late 1600s, Virginia colonists began exploring Kentucky. The French were also interested in Kentucky and were the first Europeans to claim the land.

Both Britain and France claimed Kentucky and other western lands. In 1754, these conflicting claims led to the French and Indian War. Britain won the war in 1763 and France gave up its claims. However, Native Americans kept fighting British settlers. King George III issued the Proclamation of 1763. It said that British settlers must leave all lands west of the Appalachian Mountains. This land was for Native Americans. British colonists, however, ignored the Proclamation. Pioneers poured into Kentucky and started settlements.

In 1775, the American Revolution began. British soldiers encouraged Native Americans to attack Kentucky settlements. Settlers gathered in forts to defend themselves. The United States won its independence. Fighting ended in 1783.

After the war, more settlers came to Kentucky. Kentucky became a state in 1792.

Read the summary above. Then answer the questions that follow.

1. A proclamation is—
   A a gift of land
   B a sudden, great change
   C a land ruled by a distant country
   D an order from a country's leader to its citizens

2. What happened after the French and Indian War?
   A British settlers left Kentucky.
   B France gave up its claim to Kentucky.
   C Virginia colonists began exploring Kentucky.
   D Native Americans stopped attacking settlers.

3. A pioneer is—
   A a friend in war
   B a volunteer army
   C an official population count
   D a person who first settles in a new place

4. When did Kentucky become a state?
   A 1792
   B 1783
   C 1775
   D 1763

5. How did the Cumberland Gap promote the settlement of Kentucky?

6. What rights did the Treaty of Camp Charlotte give Kentucky settlers?

7. Who was John Finley?

8. In what ways did Daniel Boone take part in the American Revolution?

9 How is George Rogers Clark important to Kentucky history?

10. Why did new settlers come to Kentucky after the Revolutionary War?

Write the letter of the best choice.

11. What was the first permanent European settlement in Kentucky?
   A Boonesborough
   B Harrodsburg
   C Logan's Station
   D Lexington

12. Who was Kentucky's first teacher?
   A Ann McGinty
   B Simon Kenton
   C Richard Henderson
   D Jane Coomes

13. How did most Kentucky pioneers earn a living?
   A by farming
   B by trading
   C by working at a job
   D by joining the army

14. Who is known as the "Father of the First Kentucky Constitution"?
   A Daniel Boone
   B Benjamin Logan
   C George Nicholas
   D Isaac Shelby

15. How did the interaction of different groups of people affect Kentucky's development as a frontier land?

Skills

Use an Elevation Map

Use the map on page 69 to answer this question.

16. What is the elevation around Paducah?

 **OPEN-RESPONSE**

Writing Task 1

Situation: You are a Kentucky historian who has been asked to do a presentation about Kentucky's early cultures.

Writing Task: Gather information about the cultures of Kentucky's Native Americans and early settlers. Write a speech that tells about what was similar and what was different about each group's way of life.

Writing Task 2

Situation: Your friend in Scotland knows little about what life is like in Kentucky today. She is wondering what your school is like and what schools were like in the past.

Writing Task: In an e-mail message to your friend, describe Kentucky's first school in Harrodsburg and how students learned there. Then tell her about how education has changed since that time.

 For more resources, go to
www.harcourtschool.com/ss1

Whose T-Shirt

See if you can match these people with the right T-shirts.

BOONESBOROUGH
GOTTA LOVE THE NAME!

NUMBER 1 TEACHER

I've been to VINCENNES ...TWICE!

I MADE THIS T SHIRT

Government PLANNER

I WALKED THE GAP

THERE'S A BURG with MY NAME ON IT!

I FOUGHT AT LITTLE MOUNTAIN

Progress as a State

 Start with the Standards

Kentucky Core Content for Assessment

SS-04-2.2.1 Students will describe social institutions in Kentucky and how they respond to the needs of the people.

SS-04-2.3.2 Students will give examples of conflicts between individuals or groups today and describe appropriate conflict resolution strategies to use.

SS-04-3.1.1 Students will describe scarcity and explain how scarcity requires people in Kentucky to make economic choices and incur opportunity costs.

SS-04-3.3.1 Students will give examples of markets; explain how they function and how the prices of goods and services are determined by supply and demand.

SS-04-3.4.1 Students will describe production, distribution and consumption of goods and services in regions of Kentucky and the U.S.

SS-04-3.4.2 Students will describe how new knowledge, technology/tools and specialization increases productivity and promotes trade between regions of Kentucky and the United States.

SS-04-4.1.3 Students will describe how different factors influence where human activities were/are located in Kentucky.

SS-04-4.3.1 Students will describe patterns of human settlement in regions of Kentucky and explain how these patterns were/are influenced by physical characteristics.

SS-04-4.3.2 Students will describe how advances in technology allow people to settle in places previously inaccessible in Kentucky.

SS-04-5.1.1 Students will use a variety of primary and secondary sources to describe significant events in the history of Kentucky and interpret different perspectives.

SS-04-5.2.2 Students will identify and compare the cultures of diverse groups and explain why people explored and settled Kentucky.

SS-04-5.2.3 Students will compare change over time in communication, technology, transportation and education in Kentucky.

The Big Idea

Growth and Change

Historical events and human activities have caused Kentucky to grow and change over time.

What to Know

✓ What changes happened in Kentucky after it became a state?

✓ What happened in Kentucky during the Civil War?

✓ How was life in Kentucky different after the Civil War?

✓ How did Kentucky change in the first half of the twentieth century?

✓ What events changed Kentucky after World War II?

✓ In what ways has Kentucky continued to change?

Time

Progress as a State

1818 The Jackson Purchase expands Kentucky borders, p. 107

1880 Kentucky has more than 1,500 miles of railroad, p. 121

1800

1870

At the Same Time

1861 The Civil War begins

1830 The Indian Removal Act forces Native Americans out of the southern United States into the southwest region

Progress as a State

1940

Present

1963 Dr. Martin Luther King, Jr., leads a civil rights march in Washington, D.C.

1941 The United States enters World War II

1930s The Dust Bowl begins in the west and southwest regions of the United States

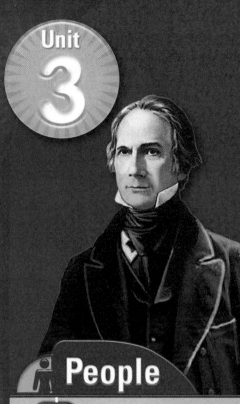

Henry Clay

1777–1852
- U.S. Senator from Kentucky known as the "Great Compromiser"
- Tried to prevent the Civil War
- Freed his enslaved workers

John James Audubon

1785–1851
- Famous naturalist
- Traveled Kentucky and documented its wildlife, especially birds
- Published his drawings in *Birds of America*

People

1760	1810	1860

- 1777 • Henry Clay — 1852
- 1785 • John James Audubon — 1851
- 1814? • William Wells Brown — 1884
- 1846 • Carry Nation
- 1856 • Louis Brandeis
- 1872 •

Louis Brandeis

1856–1941
- One of 11 Kentuckians to serve as a United States Supreme Court Justice
- Served from 1916 until 1939
- The first Jewish American to serve on the Supreme Court

Madeline McDowell Breckinridge

1872–1920
- Worked for women's right to vote
- Helped start schools, parks, and clinics for the poor

William Wells Brown

1814?–1884

- First famous African-American novelist
- Escaped from slavery in 1834
- Wrote books about his experiences as an enslaved person

Carry Nation

1846–1911

- Worked to make alcoholic beverages illegal
- Supported equal rights for women
- Supported many charities

1910   **1960**   **Present**

1911

1941

Madeline McDowell Breckinridge 1920

1911 • Bill Monroe   1996

1921 • Whitney M. Young, Jr.   1971

Bill Monroe

1911–1996

- Often called "The Father of Bluegrass Music"
- First radio performance in 1927
- Sold more than 25 million records

Whitney M. Young, Jr.

1921–1971

- Served in the U.S. Army during World War II
- Worked for civil rights for African Americans during the Civil Rights movement
- Received the Presidential Medal of Freedom in 1969

Place

Kentucky, 1860

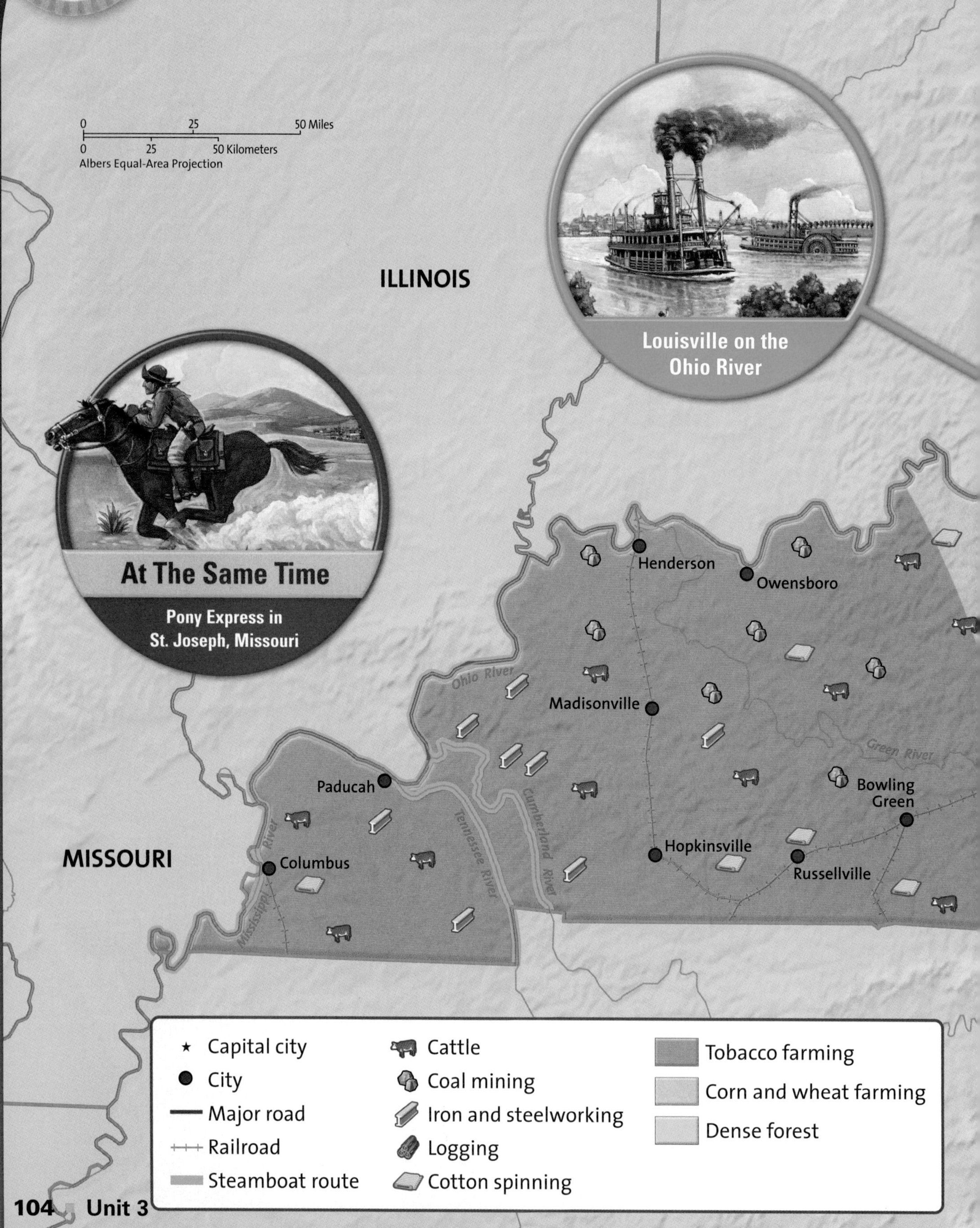

Louisville on the Ohio River

At The Same Time

Pony Express in St. Joseph, Missouri

0   25   50 Miles
0   25   50 Kilometers
Albers Equal-Area Projection

ILLINOIS

MISSOURI

Henderson
Owensboro
Madisonville
Paducah
Columbus
Hopkinsville
Bowling Green
Russellville

Ohio River
Green River
Tennessee River
Cumberland River
Mississippi River

★	Capital city		Cattle		Tobacco farming
●	City		Coal mining		Corn and wheat farming
—	Major road		Iron and steelworking		Dense forest
++++	Railroad		Logging		
	Steamboat route		Cotton spinning		

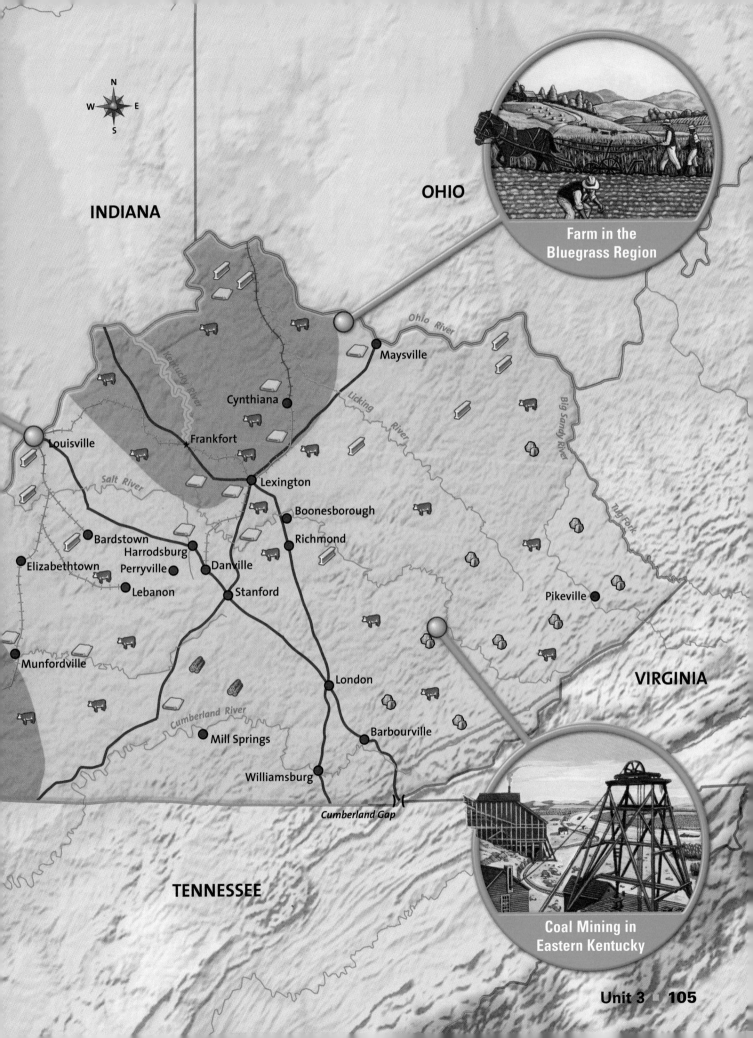

INDIANA

OHIO

Farm in the
Bluegrass Region

Ohio River

Maysville

Cynthiana

Frankfort

Louisville

Salt River

Kentucky River

Licking River

Lexington

Boonesborough

Richmond

Bardstown
Harrodsburg

Danville

Elizabethtown
Perryville

Lebanon

Stanford

Munfordville

Big Sandy River

Tug Fork

Pikeville

VIRGINIA

London

Cumberland River

Mill Springs

Barbourville

Williamsburg

Cumberland Gap

Coal Mining in
Eastern Kentucky

TENNESSEE

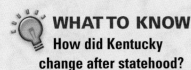
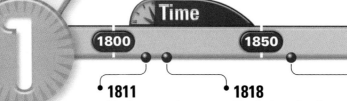

Time

1800   **1850**   **1900**

1811
The first steamboat travels on the Ohio River

1818
The Jackson Purchase expands Kentucky's borders

1860
More than 1 million people live in Kentucky

WHAT TO KNOW
How did Kentucky change after statehood?

VOCABULARY
expedition p. 107
navigable p. 108
steamboat p. 108
stagecoach p. 108
surplus p. 109
industry p. 110
textile p. 110

PEOPLE
Henry Clay
William Clark
Thomas Jefferson
Meriwether Lewis
Cyrus McCormick
John Deere

PLACES
Louisville
Lexington

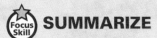
SUMMARIZE

Growing and Changing

YOU ARE THERE

"Here it comes!" you and your friend yell at the same time. You are standing on the bank of the Ohio River. A big riverboat chugs around the bend. Black smoke pours from its chimneys. You and your friend wave your hats in the air. People wave back at you from the big boat's decks.

"Someday, I'm going to be a riverboat captain," your friend says.

"Me, too!" you answer.

A Thriving State

After statehood, people poured into Kentucky. By 1800, more than 200,000 called Kentucky home. A few Kentucky leaders became famous throughout the nation.

Kentucky Leaders

Henry Clay represented Kentucky in Congress and even ran for President. He was famous for his ability to get opposing sides to agree to compromises. Because of this skill, he is remembered as the Great Compromiser.

William Clark was another famous Kentuckian. In 1803, President **Thomas Jefferson** chose Clark and **Meriwether Lewis** to lead an

important expedition. An **expedition** is a journey of exploration.

Lewis and Clark explored the Louisiana Purchase. It was a vast area of the West that the United States had just purchased from France. The group had met and planned the trip at the Falls of the Ohio River, near **Louisville**. Of the 30 or so members of the group who traveled with Lewis and Clark, 9 were Kentuckians.

New Land

In 1818, Kentucky grew by buying land from the Chickasaw. This region between the Mississippi River and the Tennessee River is often called the Jackson Purchase.

READING CHECK ☼**SUMMARIZE**
What role did Kentuckians play in the Lewis and Clark expedition?

▶ **TRAVELING** An early steamboat sails down the Ohio River (below). William Clark made this sketch of a trout (above) in his travel journal.

New Ways to Travel

New ways to travel helped Kentucky grow. On both rivers and roads, travel became faster and easier.

Better Boats

Many of Kentucky's rivers are **navigable**. That means they are deep and wide enough for large boats to use. Most of the state's large towns grew up along navigable rivers.

In the late 1700s and early 1800s, different kinds of boats brought more people and goods to Kentucky. Flatboats were often used. They could carry large loads even in shallow water.

Flatboats could not easily travel upstream, however. They were too heavy to be paddled against most river currents. Steamboats provided the power needed to travel upstream.

A **steamboat** is a boat powered by a steam engine that turns a large paddle wheel. As the wheel turns, it pushes the steamboat through the water.

The first steamboat reached the Ohio River in 1811. Over the years, steamboats continued to improve and became larger, faster, and safer. Kentucky cities all along the river grew because of steamboats. The biggest port on the river was Louisville.

On the Road

Lexington was one of the few cities that was not near a river. Beginning in 1803, stagecoaches linked Lexington to other cities by roads. A **stagecoach** is an enclosed wagon that carried passengers and was pulled by horses.

READING CHECK ☼ **SUMMARIZE**
What changes did steamboat travel bring?

Steamboats became larger and traveled faster than earlier steamboats.

Farming Changes

Change soon came to Kentucky's farms, too. In fact, new farm machines changed life not only on farms but also in cities.

More Food with Less Work

In 1831, a man from Virginia named **Cyrus McCormick** invented the mechanical reaper for harvesting wheat and other grains. With this invention, farmers could harvest as much grain in one day as they had been able to harvest in two weeks using hand tools.

In 1837, a threshing machine was invented. A thresher separated the grains from the plant stems. In that same year, **John Deere** developed the first cast-steel plow, which made tilling the soil easier. These inventions also sped up farmwork.

New farm machines meant that farmers could plant larger crops and harvest more food. Many Kentucky farmers began to produce surpluses of crops. A **surplus** is an extra amount.

Money to Spend

Crop surpluses changed farmers' lives. Farmers sold their surpluses. For the first time, many farmers had money to spend. They were able to buy goods they could not make themselves, such as farm machines, kitchen utensils, and sewing equipment.

Businesses that made and sold these goods began to grow. Many of those businesses were in cities. As a result, new ways of farming helped Kentucky cities grow.

READING CHECK 🖎 **SUMMARIZE**
How did new farm machines change life in Kentucky?

Changes in Travel and Farming

ILLUSTRATION By the mid-1800s, the way people traveled and the way land was farmed had changed greatly. Do you think it was faster to travel by steamboat or by wagon?

The McCormick reaper allowed farmers to harvest grain much faster than before.

Horse-drawn wagons carried passengers from city to city.

New Industries

New industries grew to provide the products and services that people wanted to buy. An **industry** is all the businesses that make one kind of product or provide one kind of service.

Flour and Salt

Flour mills provided a necessary service. Farmers took their grain to mills to be ground into flour. Many mills were built along rivers and streams. They used the water current to power the mills. Other mills used horses to turn stones that ground the grain.

Another industry developed to make salt. In some parts of Kentucky, people drilled deep wells to reach underground salt water. They boiled the water until only salt was left.

Other Industries

Most Kentucky households used gunpowder in guns for hunting and protection on the frontier. Many caves contained deposits of saltpeter, an ingredient used to make gunpowder. Gunpowder mills started in cities near such caves. In 1810, there were six gunpowder mills in Lexington.

Other industries used iron to make plows, kettles, and other products. Workers throughout the South wore clothing made from **textiles**, or cloth, woven in Kentucky's textile mills. Textile mills were powered by steam engines.

A Textile Mill

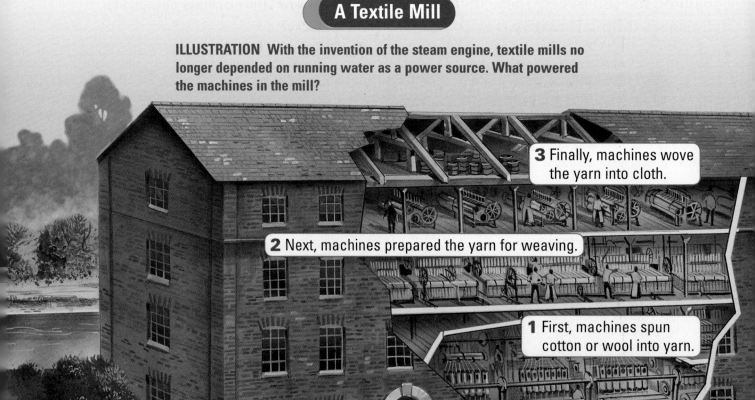

ILLUSTRATION With the invention of the steam engine, textile mills no longer depended on running water as a power source. What powered the machines in the mill?

3 Finally, machines wove the yarn into cloth.

2 Next, machines prepared the yarn for weaving.

1 First, machines spun cotton or wool into yarn.

A Wilderness No More

Between 1800 and 1860, Kentucky's population grew from about 200,000 to more than 1 million. During these years, the state began to look very different. Villages were growing into towns and cities.

READING CHECK ☼**SUMMARIZE**
What were some early industries in Kentucky?

Kentucky Population Growth

YEAR	POPULATION
1790	73,077
1800	220,955
1810	406,509
1820	564,135
1830	687,917
1840	779,828
1850	982,405
1860	1,155,684

Summary

In the years after statehood, much growth and change happened in Kentucky. The population grew quickly, and the Jackson Purchase expanded the state's borders. New transportation, farm machines, and industries helped Kentucky's cities grow and changed people's lives.

The steam engine turned the gears that drove the different machines inside the mill.

REVIEW

1. **WHAT TO KNOW** How did Kentucky change after statehood?

2. **VOCABULARY** Use the words **steamboat** and **stagecoach** to describe how transportation changed.

3. **HISTORY** What Kentuckian became a famous explorer of the West?

4. **CRITICAL THINKING** How do you think new, faster ways of travel changed people's ways of life in Kentucky?

5. ✎ **WRITE AN ADVERTISEMENT** Write a newspaper advertisement for a steamboat company or a stagecoach line. Tell why travelers should use your company to travel in Kentucky.

6. (Focus Skill) **SUMMARIZE** On a separate sheet of paper, copy and complete the graphic organizer below.

Key Fact	Summary
Beginning in 1811, steamboats made river travel faster and easier in Kentucky.	
Beginning in 1803, stagecoaches improved travel by road.	

Time

1861
The Civil War begins

1862
The Battle of Perryville is the deadliest Civil War battle in Kentucky

1865
The Union wins the Civil War

WHAT TO KNOW
What role did Kentucky play in the Civil War?

VOCABULARY
civil war p. 113
slavery p. 113
slave state p. 113
free state p. 113
abolitionist p. 113
secede p. 113
border state p. 114
neutral p. 114

PEOPLE
Abraham Lincoln
General Robert E. Lee
General Ulysses S. Grant

PLACES
Mill Springs
Richmond
Frankfort
Lexington
Perryville
Appomattox Court House

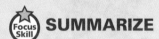

SUMMARIZE

Key Facts   Summary

Kentucky During the Civil War

YOU ARE THERE

The year is 1861. War is tearing apart your country and your state—even your family.

Your father is ready to fight for the Union. Your uncle is just as ready to fight for the Confederacy. All across Kentucky, brothers are preparing to fight against brothers. It is a terrible time.

▶ **ABRAHAM LINCOLN** was born in Kentucky. He spoke out against slavery, but was determined to keep the United States together.

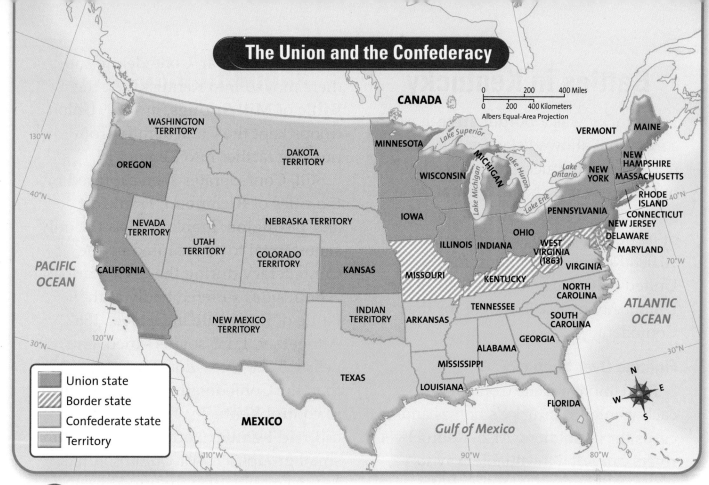

The Union and the Confederacy

Legend:
- Union state
- Border state
- Confederate state
- Territory

MAP SKILL LOCATION In the Civil War, the Northern states fought against the Southern states. Which states were border states?

North and South

In 1861, conflicts between Northern states and Southern states led to civil war. A **civil war** is a war between two groups in the same country.

Slavery

The main conflict was over **slavery**, the practice of treating people as property. The Southern states were **slave states**. Many Southerners depended on the work of enslaved people. The Northern states were **free states**, where slavery was against the law. Many Northerners were **abolitionists**. They wanted slavery to be outlawed in the South, too.

Kentuckians did not agree on the issue of slavery. Some had brought enslaved Africans with them when they settled in Kentucky. In 1860, about one-fifth of all Kentuckians were enslaved.

The Nation Divides

In 1860, **Abraham Lincoln** was elected President. Many Southerners thought Lincoln would try to end slavery. For this reason, 11 slave states **seceded** from, or left, the United States. They formed a new country, the Confederate States of America, or the Confederacy. In 1861, the two sides went to war.

READING CHECK ☼SUMMARIZE
What caused the Civil War?

Battles in Kentucky

Kentucky was a **border state**— a state that allowed slavery but did not secede. Kentucky hoped to stay out of the war by being **neutral**, or not picking a side. However, many of its people did pick a side. About 90,000 Kentuckians fought for the United States, also known then as the Union. About 40,000 fought for the Confederacy.

Fighting Over Kentucky

The Union and the Confederacy each wanted Kentucky's horses and crops for its soldiers. Also, Kentucky's rivers provided a valuable way to move soldiers and supplies. Both sides wanted to control Kentucky.

Early in the war, Confederate soldiers moved into Kentucky. At the Battle of **Mill Springs**, in 1862, Union troops kept the Confederates from pushing farther into Kentucky.

Still, Confederates soon captured the cities of **Richmond**, **Frankfort**, and **Lexington**. Frankfort was the only state capital to be captured by the Confederacy during the Civil War.

Both sides suffered badly at the Battle of **Perryville** in October 1862. Altogether, 1,355 soldiers died, and nearly 5,500 were wounded. After that, the Confederates gave up trying to control Kentucky. However, they did raid Kentucky often and fought in small groups against Union soldiers. Many small battles continued in Kentucky until the war's end.

 MAP SKILL **MOVEMENT** During the Civil War, both sides wanted to control Kentucky. Which battles were Union victories?

MAJOR CIVIL WAR BATTLES IN KENTUCKY

Union victory
Confederate victory
State capital

Cincinnati
CYNTHIANA
Louisville
Frankfort
Lexington
Ohio River
MIDDLE CREEK
PERRYVILLE
RICHMOND
IVY MOUNTAIN
MUNFORDVILLE
CAMP WILDCAT
Mississippi River
PADUCAH
MILL SPRINGS
BARBOURVILLE
Columbus
Bowling Green
Cumberland Gap

PERRYVILLE October 8, 1862

N
W   E
S

▶ **THE SURRENDER** This painting shows General Lee (seated at left) surrendering to General Grant (seated at right) in Appomattox Court House.

The Union won the Civil War in 1865. On April 9, Confederate **General Robert E. Lee** surrendered to Union **General Ulysses S. Grant** at **Appomattox Court House**, Virginia. More than 600,000 soldiers had died.

READING CHECK ⌚**SUMMARIZE**

Why did both the Union and the Confederacy want to control Kentucky?

Summary

In 1861, conflicts between the North and the South led to the Civil War. Kentucky was a border state, and Kentuckians fought on both sides. Kentucky's valuable resources made it the site of many battles. The Union won the Civil War in 1865.

REVIEW

1. **WHAT TO KNOW** What role did Kentucky play in the Civil War?

2. **VOCABULARY** How did **border states** differ from **free states**?

3. **HISTORY** Why did 11 Southern states secede from the United States?

4. **CRITICAL THINKING** How did Kentucky's location affect its role in the Civil War?

5. **WRITE A JOURNAL ENTRY** Imagine that you live in Kentucky in 1861 and that your family members have taken different sides in the war. Write a journal entry about how this has affected your lives.

6. **SUMMARIZE** On a separate sheet of paper, copy and complete the graphic organizer below.

Key Fact	Summary
Kentucky had navigable rivers that could be used to move soldiers and supplies.	
Kentucky had crops and horses that soldiers needed.	

FIELD TRIP

READ ABOUT

Civil War Heritage Trail

The Kentucky Civil War Heritage Trail was created to give Kentuckians an exciting way to learn about their past. Historical sites across the state team up each year to teach about the Civil War.

On the Heritage Trail, guides take visitors on tours of Kentucky's major battlefields. Visitors learn about what happened at each battle. People can visit museums, watch Civil War-style cannons fire, and even eat a Civil War-era meal! People who go on the Civil War Heritage Trail have an experience like none other.

FIND

UNION SOLDIERS Re-enactors play Union soldiers in Georgetown, Kentucky.

LINCOLN'S BIRTHPLACE

JEFFERSON DAVIS' BIRTHPLACE

RE-ENACTORS PERFORMING AS CONFEDERATE SOLDIERS

UNION HEADQUARTERS

CAMP NELSON CEMETERY

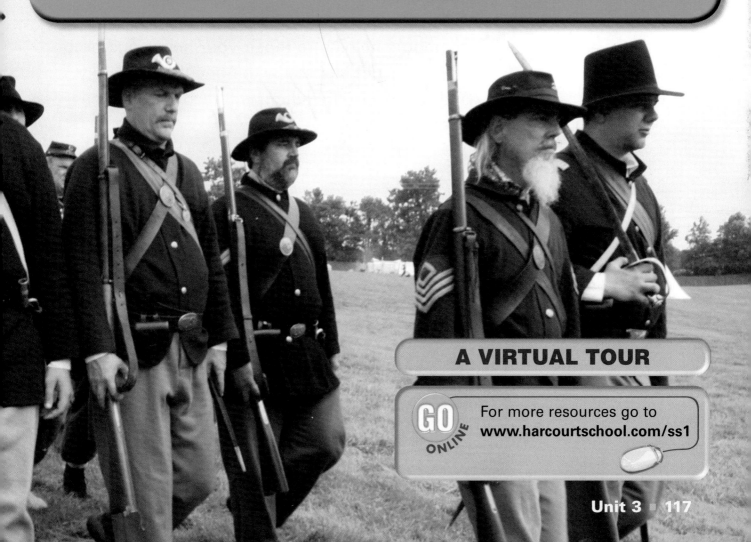

A VIRTUAL TOUR

GO **ONLINE** For more resources go to www.harcourtschool.com/ss1

Time

| 1800 | 1850 | 1900 |

1865
The Thirteenth Amendment ends slavery in Kentucky

1880
Kentucky has more than 1,500 miles of railroads

1892
Kentucky celebrates its centennial as a state

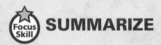

WHAT TO KNOW
How did life in Kentucky change after the Civil War?

VOCABULARY
sharecropping p. 120
locomotive p. 121
manufacturing p. 122
centennial p. 123

SUMMARIZE

Key Facts	Summary

Kentucky After the Civil War

YOU ARE THERE

The year is 1865. You have just returned home to Kentucky from fighting in the war. You are relieved that those terrible years are over. Yet many new challenges lie ahead. The Union has been preserved, but at a great cost.

As you walk up to your home, you see your neighbors helping to repair your house and property. The sight fills you with hope that Kentucky and the rest of the nation will recover from the effects of war.

The Costs of War

The Civil War was over. While the war's end was welcome, Kentucky had suffered many losses.

Much to Rebuild

More than 600,000 soldiers died in the Civil War. About 30,000 of them were from Kentucky. Hundreds of thousands of animals had died or were taken during the war. These included horses, mules, and cattle. After the war, Kentuckians needed these animals for transportation, farmwork, and food.

Many buildings, railroads, and bridges were destroyed during the war. Also, crops had gone unplanted while men were away fighting.

People faced the job of rebuilding their homes, farms, and businesses. It was a difficult time to earn a living. Few people in the South had money to buy things. As a result, farmers and shop owners found few customers for their crops and products.

Hard Feelings

Many Kentuckians who had fought on opposite sides during the war remained bitter toward their former enemies. Hard feelings divided families and communities. These feelings made it hard for people to work together to rebuild Kentucky.

READING CHECK **SUMMARIZE**
What losses did Kentucky suffer in the Civil War?

❯ **COMING HOME** A Union soldier returns to his home in Kentucky.

Slavery Ends

During the war, President Lincoln had issued the Emancipation Proclamation. It declared that enslaved people in Confederate states were free. Kentucky was not part of the Confederacy, however. Its enslaved people were not yet free.

Slaves Become Sharecroppers

In December 1865, the Thirteenth Amendment to the Constitution ended slavery everywhere in the United States. Kentucky's 225,000 enslaved people were now free.

People who had been enslaved should have been free to live as they chose. However, most of them had few choices. Most had little or no money. Few could read or write.

Landowners still needed workers to plant and harvest crops. As a result, many formerly enslaved people continued to do the same work they had done before they were free. However, landowners now had to pay their workers.

Few people had money, so many landowners paid workers in shares of crops. This system was known as **sharecropping**. A landowner provided housing and supplies to a worker, called a sharecropper. The sharecropper farmed the land. At harvest time, the landowner took some of the crops for himself and as payment for the worker's housing and supplies. The sharecropper got just enough to survive.

READING CHECK ☼**SUMMARIZE**
What is the Thirteenth Amendment?

Children IN HISTORY

Malinda Robinson Paris

Malinda Robinson was born in Paris, Kentucky, in 1824. Malinda's father was enslaved, but her mother was a free woman. Slave owners tried to force Malinda and her brothers and sisters into slavery. To protect the children, Malinda's mother took them to Indiana, a free state. They traveled on the Underground Railroad. This was a system of secret routes that enslaved people used to escape from slave states.

Malinda later married William Paris and moved to Michigan. Her son Henry served on the Union side during the Civil War.

Make It Relevant **How did Malinda's mother protect her children?**

▶ **RAILROADS** were not just a great way to get around Kentucky—they were a big industry. People could buy railroad company shares (left) and earn profits.

Railroads

Railroads helped Kentucky rebuild and grow after the Civil War. When the war ended in 1865, the state had fewer than 600 miles of track. By 1880, the number had grown to more than 1,500 miles of track. From 1880 to 1900, the number doubled to 3,000 miles.

Trains Connect Kentuckians

The first railroad cars in the United States were pulled by horses. In 1830, the first steam-powered **locomotive**, or railroad engine, was built. Soon locomotives replaced horses, just as steamboats had replaced flatboats.

In Kentucky, railroads provided a way for people in all parts of the state to ship crops and products to buyers. The first railroad in Kentucky began in 1832 and was called the Lexington and Ohio Railroad. When the railroad came to a small town, it brought new opportunities for farmers and others to sell their products.

Trains carried people as well as products. A trip of 100 miles could take days on horseback but only half a day by train. Kentuckians began traveling farther to visit friends and family members and also to do business.

READING CHECK ⚙ **SUMMARIZE**
How did railroads change life in Kentucky?

Coal Is King

Railroads needed coal to run their steam-powered locomotives. Other industries needed coal, too. Many people needed coal to heat their homes. As a result, coal became big business in Kentucky.

Factories Burn Coal

Steelmaking was one of the new industries that needed coal. Coal-burning furnaces melted iron ore so it could be mixed with other ingredients to make steel—a material that was stronger than iron. **Manufacturing**, or the making of products, also required coal. Many factories used coal to run machines that made products ranging from farming tools to kitchen utensils.

A Booming Business

As industries grew, the demand for coal increased. As a result, the coal-mining industry boomed, or experienced a sudden rapid growth.

In 1870, miners brought 150,000 tons of coal out of Kentucky mines. Only ten years later, Kentucky was producing more than 1 million tons of coal every year.

Many people who had been farmers got jobs as coal miners. Railroads carried Kentucky's coal to all parts of the state and beyond.

> **COAL MINERS** Workers for the Gaines Coal Company used mules to haul loads of coal out of the mine. To see in the dark mine shafts, they used special coal mine lanterns like the one above.

FAST FACT

In 1870, about 1,200 Kentuckians worked in coal mines. By the early 1900s, that number grew to more than 10,000. Today, more than 15,000 people work in the Kentucky coal mining industry.

WOMAN'S SUFFRAGE Laura Clay and other Kentucky women march for the right to vote, at a convention in St. Louis, Missouri.

Women Win the Vote

In 1919, American women did not have **suffrage**, or the right to vote in national and other elections. Some women had been fighting for that right for many years.

Madeline Breckinridge

One Kentuckian who worked for woman's suffrage was **Madeline Breckinridge**. She was the great-granddaughter of Henry Clay, who had represented Kentucky in Congress.

In the early 1900s, Breckinridge turned her attention to women's right to vote. She gave speeches in support of the Nineteenth Amendment to the Constitution. This amendment would give all women the right to vote if enough states approved it.

LAURA CLAY

Laura Clay

Like Breckinridge, **Laura Clay** worked for woman's suffrage. She was the daughter of abolitionist Cassius Marcellus Clay. Madeline Breckinridge and Laura Clay were the first women to give speeches to both houses of the Kentucky legislature.

Because of their efforts, the legislature voted for the Nineteenth Amendment on January 6, 1920. Later that year, the required number of states approved the amendment. For the first time, American women could vote in all elections.

READING CHECK SUMMARIZE

Why are Breckinridge and Clay remembered?

A New Industry

A new industry grew in Kentucky in the early 1900s. It would change life for Kentuckians and for all Americans.

Henry Ford and the Model T

Henry Ford was one of the most important entrepreneurs of the twentieth century. An **entrepreneur** (ahn•truh•pruh•NER) sets up and runs a business.

Ford's business was making automobiles, or cars. He started his business in Michigan but soon built factories in Kentucky.

The first Kentucky car factory opened in Louisville in 1913. It had only 17 workers and made 12 cars each day. By 1925, though, a much larger factory made 400 cars a day.

Ford's factories were just the beginning of the automobile industry in Kentucky. Today, several companies manufacture automobiles in Kentucky factories.

Cars gave people the freedom to travel more. People were no longer limited by train routes and schedules.

State Parks

Soon after the automobile came to Kentucky, the legislature set up a State Parks Commission. Many important natural and historical sites became state parks that welcomed visitors from Kentucky and around the nation. **Cumberland Falls State Resort Park** and **Fort Boonesborough State Park** were among the most popular.

READING CHECK ☉SUMMARIZE
How did cars change people's lives?

❯ **MODEL Ts** A Model T rolls off the assembly line (left) at the Ford factory in Louisville. Many Kentuckians owned automobiles in the 1920s (below).

▶ **THE GREAT DEPRESSION** Many Americans waited in bread lines (above) to get food during the Depression. A young Kentuckian (right) drinks a bottle of milk he received in a relief lunch program.

Boom and Bust

During the 1920s, many Americans lived well. New industries, including the automobile industry, provided good jobs. People had more money to spend on things that made life easier and more fun, ranging from telephones to movie tickets.

The Great Depression

Then, all of a sudden, everything changed. In the fall of 1929, the Great Depression began. A **depression** is a time when there are few jobs and people have little money.

The Great Depression was a terrible time throughout the United States, including in Kentucky. Businesses closed because few people had money to buy their products and services. As a result, people lost their jobs. **Unemployment**, or the number of workers without jobs, was as high as one of every four workers.

Workers without jobs could not pay their bills. Some people lost their houses. Others lost all their savings when banks failed.

The United States government started programs to provide jobs. In Kentucky, more than 140,000 people worked at government jobs. Some built cabins and trails in state parks. Others built schools, roads, and bridges.

The Tennessee Valley Authority (TVA) was another United States government program. In this program, workers built dams in Kentucky and in nearby states. The dams controlled flooding and produced electricity for the region.

READING CHECK Ŏ**SUMMARIZE**
How did the Great Depression affect Kentucky?

World War II

In 1939, World War II began in Europe. The war came to the United States on December 7, 1941. On that day, Japanese airplanes bombed American ships at Pearl Harbor, in Hawaii.

Kentucky Soldiers

More than 306,000 Kentuckians served in World War II. **Admiral Husband Kimmel**, who commanded the fleet at Pearl Harbor, was from Kentucky. So was **Admiral Willis A. Lee**, who commanded battleships in the Pacific Ocean. **General Simon B. Buckner** led American forces at the Battle of Okinawa, Japan. General Buckner was one of almost 8,000 Kentuckians who died in the war.

The nation needed food and supplies for soldiers. In fact, war needs led to shortages at home. A **shortage** is a lack of something. During World War II, Americans faced shortages of meat, butter, sugar, gasoline, and other products.

Kentuckians joined other Americans in trying to reduce shortages. They limited their use of products in short supply. Many started vegetable gardens to lessen food shortages. People collected scrap metal that could be made into weapons and equipment.

Businesses, too, did their part to supply the troops. The Ford Motor Company factory in Louisville made nearly 100,000 jeeps for the Army. The Louisville Slugger factory, which made baseball bats before the war, made rifles in wartime.

❯ **PEARL HARBOR** The attack by the Japanese brought the United States into World War II.

With many men away at war, women took factory jobs for the first time. They did very important work to help the war effort. By creating jobs, World War II helped end the Great Depression. The United States and its allies won the war in 1945.

READING CHECK **⭮SUMMARIZE**
How did World War II change people's lives in Kentucky?

Summary

Kentucky and the nation experienced both good times and challenges in the first half of the twentieth century. Kentuckians served in World War I and in World War II. They helped American women win the right to vote, and they overcame the hardships of the Great Depression.

▶ **WORKING WOMEN** This woman (above) worked in a factory in Kentucky that made bullets during the war. Posters of "Rosie the Riveter" (right) encouraged women to help in the war effort.

REVIEW

1. **WHAT TO KNOW** What events affected Kentucky in the first half of the twentieth century?

2. **VOCABULARY** What happens during a **depression**?

3. **HISTORY** How did United States government programs help Kentucky during the Great Depression?

4. **CRITICAL THINKING** How do you think working different jobs during World War II changed women's lives?

5. **MAKE AN ILLUSTRATED TIME LINE**
   Make an illustrated time line that shows the major events that happened in Kentucky and in the United States between 1900 and 1950.

6. **(Focus Skill) SUMMARIZE** On a separate sheet of paper, copy and complete the graphic organizer below.

Key Fact		Summary
Thousands of Kentuckians fought in World War I and World War II.	▶	
Kentuckians at home bought war bonds, grew vegetables, and collected scrap metal to help the war effort.	▶	

Time

1900   1950   Present

1954
The United States Supreme Court
outlaws segregation in schools

1963
The March on Washington
takes place

WHAT TO KNOW
How did Kentucky
change in the decades
after World War II?

VOCABULARY
economy p. 133
rural p. 133
urban p. 133
suburb p. 133
metropolitan area p. 133
civil rights p. 135
segregation p. 135

PEOPLE
Bill Monroe
J. D. Crowe
Ricky Skaggs
Whitney M. Young, Jr.
Martin Luther King, Jr.
President Lyndon B.
Johnson

PLACES
Owensboro
Lincoln Ridge

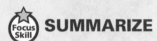
SUMMARIZE

Key Facts   Summary

Into Modern Times

YOU ARE THERE
There is no longer a
shortage of gasoline
as there was during the war. Now it seems
as if everyone is driving a new car, traveling
everywhere. You hope that today your father will
take the family in his new car to a new drive-in
restaurant in the city. You saw an advertisement
on television that showed that you can order
food at the curb and eat inside the car! Many
exciting changes are happening, now that the
war has ended.

❯ In the 1950s, Kentuckians began to have televisions
in their homes.

▶ **AFTER THE WAR** Kentucky's economy was strong after the war. The streets in the state's cities and suburbs were busy with cars and people.

Cities Grow

World War II brought plenty of jobs to Kentucky and the rest of the United States. After the war, the economy continued to grow. The **economy** is the way in which people of a state, region, or country use resources to meet their needs.

Coal Leads the Way

In the decades following the war, the population and the number of industries in the United States grew dramatically. Americans used more coal than ever before. This caused Kentucky's coal industry to grow. As a result, many people in Kentucky continued to find jobs with mining companies.

From Farms to Cities

At the same time, new factories were opening in Kentucky towns and cities. The factories made cars, chemicals, clothing, and more.

Factories meant jobs. Many people moved from **rural** areas, or areas in the country, to **urban** areas, or cities. They got jobs in factories, where they earned more money than they had earned before.

As cities grew, many suburbs grew around them. A **suburb** is a town or small city near a large city. A city together with its suburbs is called a **metropolitan area**.

READING CHECK ⟡SUMMARIZE
What was Kentucky's economy like after World War II?

Bluegrass Music

Many Kentuckians moved to cities. At the same time, the state's rural music was gaining fame.

Made in Kentucky

Early settlers in Kentucky belonged to families that had come to the United States from Scotland, Ireland, Africa, and other regions. These early settlers all brought their own forms of music to Kentucky. They mixed the different forms to create a new, made-in-Kentucky kind of music.

In 1939, Kentuckian **Bill Monroe** started a band that he named the Bluegrass Boys. They played Kentucky's music all over the United States. Soon people were calling this kind of music "bluegrass."

Bluegrass musicians play instruments such as fiddles, mandolins, and banjos. All three are stringed instruments. A mandolin sounds like a guitar but has a higher pitch.

Bill Monroe earned the nickname "The Father of Bluegrass Music." He wrote songs about Kentucky, including "Blue Moon of Kentucky."

Other famous bluegrass musicians from Kentucky include **J. D. Crowe** and **Ricky Skaggs**. The International Bluegrass Music Association is based in **Owensboro**.

READING CHECK ☼ **SUMMARIZE**
What is bluegrass music?

▶ **THE FATHER OF BLUEGRASS MUSIC** Bill Monroe (below left) performs his famous music at a festival. Monroe's music is available in numerous albums and collections (left).

Civil Rights Movement Artifacts

Background Groups used buttons and other items to help spread their messages during the Civil Rights movement.

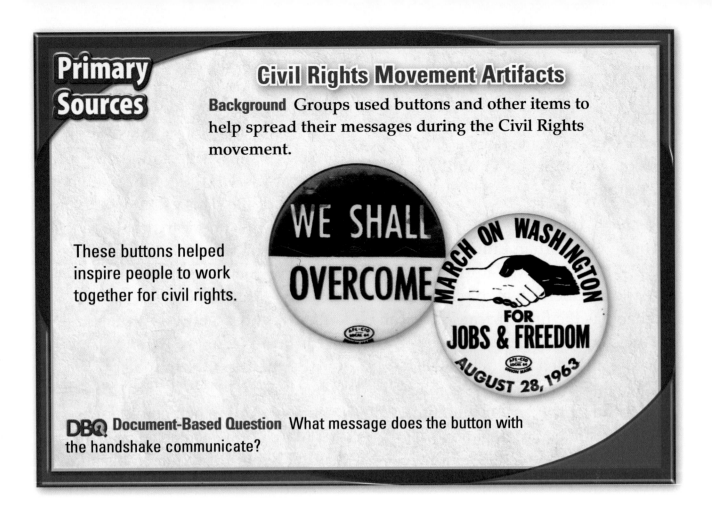

These buttons helped inspire people to work together for civil rights.

WE SHALL OVERCOME

MARCH ON WASHINGTON FOR JOBS & FREEDOM AUGUST 28, 1963

DBQ **Document-Based Question** What message does the button with the handshake communicate?

A New Movement

In the 1950s and 1960s, many African Americans and white people in the United States began to work for civil rights. **Civil rights** are the rights of citizens to equal treatment.

Working for Equal Treatment

African Americans were often treated unfairly because of their race. Some businesses refused to hire African American workers. Some banks would not lend money to African Americans who wanted to buy homes.

In many southern states, laws called for segregation. **Segregation** is the keeping of people of one race or culture separate from other people.

Many Americans began to work together to end segregation and other unfair treatment of people because of their race. This work became known as the Civil Rights movement.

As a result of the Civil Rights movement, school segregation was outlawed. In 1954, the United States Supreme Court ruled that school segregation was against the Constitution. Kentucky was the first southern state to obey the Supreme Court ruling and end school segregation.

Kentucky was also the first southern state to pass an open housing law. It said that all people had an equal right to rent or buy homes.

READING CHECK **SUMMARIZE**
What was the Civil Rights movement?

Whitney M. Young, Jr.

Many Kentuckians took part in the Civil Rights movement. One of the best-known of them was **Whitney M. Young, Jr.**

A Kentucky Leader

Young was born in **Lincoln Ridge** in 1921. His father was a principal at an African American high school. His mother was the first African American postmaster in Kentucky.

Young attended Kentucky State College in Frankfort. It was a college for African Americans. At that time, Kentucky still had segregation.

When Young wanted to continue his education, he had to move to Minnesota to do so. African Americans were not allowed to attend some Kentucky universities.

In Minnesota, Young took part in protests against segregation. In 1961, he became the leader of the National Urban League. This group worked to help African Americans get good jobs. It also encouraged all Americans to work together. Young said,

> **66** We must learn to live together as brothers or we will all surely die together as fools. **99**

In 1963, Young helped organize the March on Washington. **Martin Luther King, Jr.**, delivered his famous "I Have a Dream" speech at this event.

❯ THE MARCH ON WASHINGTON Hundreds of thousands of people marched for civil rights in the nation's capital in 1963.

▶ **AT THE WHITE HOUSE** Martin Luther King, Jr., Whitney M. Young, Jr., and other Civil Rights leaders speak with President Johnson.

Young received the Presidential Medal of Freedom from **President Lyndon B. Johnson** in 1969. It is the highest award given to Americans who are not soldiers.

READING CHECK ⓈSUMMARIZE

What is Whitney M. Young, Jr., remembered for?

Summary

After World War II, Kentucky's economy remained strong. Many people moved to cities and took jobs in factories. Many Kentuckians, including Whitney M. Young, Jr., worked for civil rights.

REVIEW

1. **WHAT TO KNOW** How did Kentucky change in the decades after World War II?

2. **VOCABULARY** How are **urban** areas and **suburbs** related?

3. **HISTORY** Who is known as "The Father of Bluegrass Music"?

4. **CRITICAL THINKING** Why do you think Whitney M. Young, Jr., chose to work for civil rights?

5. **MAKE A POSTER** Make a poster calling attention to one of the issues important to the Civil Rights movement.

6. **SUMMARIZE** On a separate sheet of paper, copy and complete the graphic organizer below.

Key Fact		Summary
Many Kentuckians left rural areas because they could earn more money in cities.	▶	
Factories provided jobs in cities.	▶	

Read a Double-Bar Graph

Why It Matters A double-bar graph shows comparisons of two or more different things. By comparing the lengths of the bars, you can quickly and easily compare the amounts they represent. The graph on page 139 shows that even though some farmers were moving to cities to take factory jobs, harvests still mostly increased in the decades following World War II.

❯ LEARN

Follow these steps to use a double-bar graph.

Step 1 Read the title of the graph on page 139. It describes the main topic of the graph. Then read the labels along the bottom and the left side. The numbers shown on the left side stand for the amounts of crops that were harvested. The years are listed along the bottom.

Step 2 Read the graph key to see what each bar stands for. The green bars stand for corn, and the purple bars stand for soybeans.

Step 3 Choose one year, and compare its two bars. In this graph, you can compare the size of the harvests of corn and soybeans in each of the six years shown.

Step 4 To find the number of bushels that a bar stands for, put your finger on the top of the bar and read the number on the left that is closest to the top of the bar.

❯ PRACTICE

Use the double-bar graph to answer these questions.

❶ About how much corn was harvested in Kentucky in 1969?

❷ Between which two years did Kentucky's corn harvest decrease?

❸ How many bushels of soybeans were harvested in 1982?

❹ Why do you think Kentucky's harvests of corn and soybeans have generally increased over the years?

❯ APPLY

Make It Relevant Make a double-bar graph of your test scores in social studies and in another subject. Remember to use a different color for each subject.

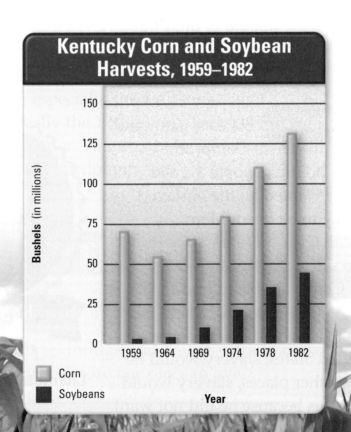

Kentucky Corn and Soybean Harvests, 1959–1982

Chart and Graph Skills

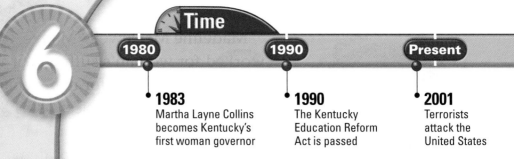

Time

1980	1990	Present

1983
Martha Layne Collins becomes Kentucky's first woman governor

1990
The Kentucky Education Reform Act is passed

2001
Terrorists attack the United States

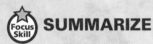 **WHAT TO KNOW**
What challenges has Kentucky faced in recent times?

VOCABULARY
high-tech p. 145
terrorist p. 146

PEOPLE
Martha Layne Collins
President George W. Bush

PLACES
New York City
Washington, D.C.

SUMMARIZE

Key Facts		Summary

Recent Times

YOU ARE THERE
You and your family are fishing in a pond in Perry County. Your mom has already caught two bass, and you have caught one. "See the geese?" your mom whispers, pointing above you. "If we're quiet, they may land nearby."

Sure enough, the birds glide down not far from you. Their honking causes a deer to raise its head above the tall grass it's eating.

"It's hard to believe that this land was once a strip mine," your mom says.

Protecting the Environment

In the 1970s, Americans were becoming more aware of the need to protect the environment. National laws affected how people and businesses in Kentucky used natural resources.

Reclaiming Land

Some of Kentucky's coal lies just beneath Earth's surface. It is removed by strip-mining. Bulldozers strip away plants and soil to reach the coal.

Strip-mining damages the land. Without soil, plants cannot grow back. Bare land can create dangerous landslides.

In 1977, the United States Congress passed a law called the Surface Mining Reclamation and Enforcement Act. It requires mining companies to reclaim strip-mined land. Under this law, tens of thousands of acres of Kentucky land have been reclaimed. Reclaimed land is being used to graze horses, to grow crops, to grow trees for timber, and to provide a home for wildlife.

Cleaning Up Pollution

The Superfund Act was another national law that affected Kentucky. It said that companies that cause pollution can be forced to pay large fines. The government uses money from fines to clean up polluted places, called Superfund sites.

Kentucky has more than a dozen Superfund sites. Most have already been cleaned up. However, much work still needs to be done.

READING CHECK ♨**SUMMARIZE**
How have national laws helped protect Kentucky's environment?

▶**KENTUCKY'S LAND** Laws help protect Kentucky's land from pollution and other hazards to the environment.

▶ **STUDENTS** in Kentucky are given the tools they need to get a good education.

Improving Education

In the late 1980s and 1990s, education was an important issue in Kentucky. The state worked hard to solve the problems that its schools were having.

A Matter of Fairness

In 1988, the Kentucky supreme court ruled that the state's public school system was breaking the law. The problem was in how state money for schools was spent. Schools in wealthy communities got more money than schools in poor communities. The supreme court said this was unfair and must be changed.

In addition, Kentucky was spending less money on education than most other states. Another problem facing Kentucky was that too many students were dropping out of high school.

The state government took action to solve these problems. In 1990, the legislature passed the Kentucky Education Reform Act (KERA). This state law provided more money for all public schools. It divided the money more fairly. It also set new standards for Kentucky students. Education in Kentucky continues to improve today.

READING CHECK ⏀ **SUMMARIZE**

How did the Kentucky Education Reform Act help improve education in Kentucky?

Welcome Changes

The last years of the twentieth century brought changes to Kentucky. They included new opportunities for women and new businesses.

Kentucky First

The first woman governor of Kentucky was **Martha Layne Collins**. She was elected in 1983 and was one of the first woman governors in the United States. Before she became active in politics, Collins was a high school teacher.

More Kentucky women were also becoming lawyers, judges, doctors, scientists, and managers. The number of Kentucky women in each of these jobs has more than tripled since 1960.

❯ **MARTHA LAYNE COLLINS**

New Businesses

Kentucky's auto industry grew as new carmaking companies came to the state. In 1993, Kentucky was the fourth-largest producer of cars in the United States.

Kentucky is also home to many other businesses. Many Kentuckians work in the health-care industry. Kentucky also has many  **high-tech** industries that invent, build, or use computers and other kinds of electronic equipment.

READING CHECK ❂ **SUMMARIZE**

Who is Martha Layne Collins?

❯ **HIGH-TECH INDUSTRIES** attract many Kentuckians, such as this medical technician.

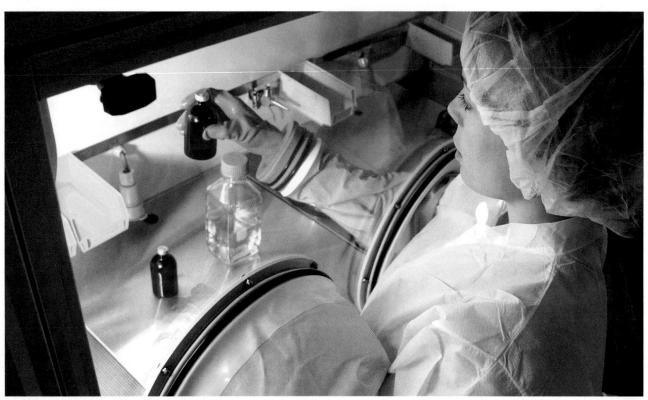

Facing New Dangers

The year 2001 marked the beginning of the twenty-first century. That year, the United States was attacked by terrorists. **Terrorists** are people who use violence to promote a cause.

An Attack Leads to War

On September 11, 2001, terrorists hijacked four American passenger planes. They crashed two planes into the twin towers of the World Trade Center in **New York City**. Both towers collapsed.

The terrorists flew the third plane into the Pentagon, the nation's military headquarters in **Washington, D.C.**

The fourth plane crashed into a field in Pennsylvania. The passengers on that plane may have fought the terrorists. Nearly 3,000 Americans died in these attacks.

United States leaders learned that many of the terrorists had been trained in Afghanistan. To end Afghanistan's support of terrorists, the United States and its allies overthrew its rulers.

In 2003, **President George W. Bush** declared that Saddam Hussein, the leader of Iraq, was a danger to the world. Along with some of its allies, the United States defeated the Iraqi army and later arrested Hussein.

➤ **THE TROOPS** at Fort Campbell, Kentucky, listen to President Bush in March 2004.

▶ **HOMELAND SECURITY** Kentucky's Director of Homeland Security is Major Alecia Webb-Edgington.

Thousands of Kentucky soldiers have already served in Afghanistan and Iraq. In a 2004 visit to Fort Campbell, President Bush said,

> **❝Many of you have seen action in the global war on terror. Some of you have just returned to Fort Campbell. . . . Thank you for a job well done.❞**

To help protect its people, Kentucky created the Kentucky Office of Homeland Security. Its purpose is to prevent terrorist attacks in Kentucky. It also helps communities and citizens prepare in case an attack occurs.

READING CHECK ⚉**SUMMARIZE**
How has the United States' response to terrorism affected Kentuckians?

Summary

The end of the twentieth century brought Kentucky's first woman governor and new businesses. The state faced challenges related to the environment and education. Since 2001, thousands of Kentuckians have served in the nation's armed forces.

REVIEW

1. **WHAT TO KNOW** What challenges has Kentucky faced in recent times?

2. **VOCABULARY** What are **high-tech** industries?

3. **HISTORY** Who was Kentucky's first woman governor?

4. **CRITICAL THINKING** How have women's roles changed in Kentucky since 1900?

5. ✏️ **WRITE A REPORT** Use library and Internet resources to write a report about a Kentuckian who is important to recent history.

6. ⭐(Focus Skill) **SUMMARIZE** On a separate sheet of paper, copy and complete the graphic organizer below.

Key Fact	Summary
Thousands of Kentucky soldiers have served in Afghanistan and Iraq. ➤	
The state established a Kentucky Office of Homeland Security to protect Kentuckians at home. ➤	

Review and Test Prep

THE BIG IDEA

Growth and Change Historical events and human activities have caused Kentucky to grow and change over time.

Reading Comprehension and Vocabulary

Progress as a State

Kentucky's population grew quickly after statehood. Flatboats, steamboats, and stagecoaches helped move people and goods to the state.

The reaper and the thresher helped Kentucky farmers produce surpluses. New businesses grew to make and sell the things people wanted to buy.

During the Civil War, Kentucky was a border state. It allowed slavery but did not secede from the Union.

After the Union won the war, slavery ended in Kentucky. Many formerly enslaved people became sharecroppers.

Railroads improved transportation and helped the coal industry boom.

Kentuckians fought in two world wars in the twentieth century. Women won the right to vote. Americans everywhere faced hardships during the Great Depression.

After World War II, many people moved from farms to cities. African Americans and others worked for civil rights.

In recent times, Kentucky has faced challenges such as protecting the environment and improving education.

Read the summary above. Then answer the questions that follow.

1. What is a surplus?
   A an extra amount
   B a journey of exploration
   C an enclosed wagon pulled by horses
   D all the businesses that make one kind of product or provide one kind of service

2. What Kentucky industry experienced a boom right after the Civil War ended?
   A the coal industry
   B the music industry
   C the automobile industry
   D the health-care industry

3. What is a depression?
   A a lack of something
   B a loan to the government
   C a person who sets up and runs a business
   D a time when there are few jobs and people have little money

4. Which of these did NOT happen during the twentieth century?
   A the Civil War
   B World War I
   C the Great Depression
   D World War II

Facts and Main Ideas

Answer these questions.

5. Why were steamboats an improvement over other boats?

6. What is the Jackson Purchase?

7. Why did both sides in the Civil War want to control Kentucky?

8. What two purposes does Fort Knox serve today?

9. Who was Bill Monroe?

10. What does the Kentucky Office of Homeland Security do?

Write the letter of the best choice.

11. Who was President of the United States during the Civil War?
    A Cassius Marcellus Clay
    B Abraham Lincoln
    C Robert E. Lee
    D Ulysses S. Grant

12. Which of the following freed all enslaved people in the United States?
    A the Thirteenth Amendment
    B the Nineteenth Amendment
    C the Emancipation Proclamation
    D the Civil Rights movement

13. What is Madeline Breckinridge remembered for?
    A She was an abolitionist.
    B She worked for woman's suffrage.
    C She led the Civil Rights movement.
    D She was Kentucky's first woman governor.

14. What is the purpose of the Superfund?
    A to prevent terrorism
    B to stop strip-mining
    C to clean up pollution
    D to improve education

Critical Thinking

15. How did advances in agricultural technology in the early 1800s strengthen Kentucky as a state?

16. How might America's involvement in World War II have helped end the Great Depression?

Skills

Read a Double-Bar Graph

Use the graph on page 139 to answer this question.

17. Between 1959 and 1982, did Kentucky harvest more bushels of corn or of soybeans?

OPEN-RESPONSE

Writing Task 1

Situation: You have visited a museum that shows the different kinds of boats that have traveled Kentucky's rivers.

Writing Task: Write an essay about how travel on Kentucky's rivers has changed throughout the state's history.

Writing Task 2

Situation: Your class has taken a trip to Washington, D.C. You visited the Lincoln Memorial, where Dr. Martin Luther King, Jr., gave his "I Have a Dream" speech.

Writing Task: Make a list of some of the demands of civil rights leaders. Then write a paragraph about the effects that the Civil Rights movement had on Kentucky and the United States.

For more resources, go to
www.harcourtschool.com/ss1

Fun with Social Studies

Match 'Em

Can you make eight matches?

Secret Identities

Each person's name is hiding in one of the words that fit the clues. Can you find them all? The letters are in order reading from left to right. The first one is done for you.

abc VOCABULARY

Cannons and other big weapons
arTILLerY

A time when there are few jobs and little money

Treating people like property

Separation of races

Water that's deep and wide enough for large boats

Someone who wants to outlaw slavery

A railroad engine

Out in the country

RON GREG GALE LIV AL TILLY AVERY LONI

Kentucky Today

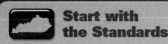
Start with the Standards

Kentucky Core Content for Assessment

SS-04-1.1.1 Students will describe the basic purposes of Kentucky government; give examples of the services that state governments provide and identify how the government of Kentucky pays for these services.

SS-04-1.1.2 Students will explain how state governments function to protect the rights and property of citizens.

SS-04-1.2.1 Students will identify the three branches of Kentucky government, explain the basic duties of each branch and identify important state offices/leaders associated with each branch.

SS-04-1.2.2 Students will explain how power is shared among the different branches of state government.

SS-04-1.3.2 Students will describe specific rights and responsibilities individuals have as citizens of Kentucky and explain why civic engagement is necessary to preserve a democratic society.

SS-04-3.2.1 Students will explain how profit motivates individuals/businesses to take risks in producing goods and services.

SS-04-3.3.1 Students will give examples of markets; explain how they function and how the prices of goods and services are determined by supply and demand.

SS-04-3.3.2 Students will explain how competition among buyers and sellers influences the price of goods and services in our state, nation and world.

SS-04-3.4.2 Students will describe how new knowledge, technology/tools and specialization increases productivity and promotes trade between regions of Kentucky and the United States.

SS-04-3.4.3 Students will define interdependence and give examples of how people in our communities, states, nation and world depend on each other for goods and services.

The Big Idea

Culture and Government

Kentuckians are proud of their culture, social institutions, and form of government.

What to Know

- Who lives in Kentucky today?
- What are the features of Kentucky's culture?
- How do Kentuckians make their living?
- How does the government of Kentucky work?
- What services do local governments provide?
- What does it mean to be a Kentuckian?

Unit 4

Kentucky has many festivals and events that help celebrate its past and present.

Shipping and transportation are important to Kentucky's economy.

Kentucky Today

Frankfort is the center of Kentucky state government.

Kentuckians can help the people of their community, state, and nation in many ways.

Unit 4

People

Dr. Thomas D. Clark

1903–2005
- Former State Historian for Kentucky
- Taught students in Kentucky and around the world

Loretta Lynn

1935–
- Country musician and one of Kentucky's most famous musical talents
- Wrote many songs about the life of working-class women, especially in the South

1903   **1924**   **1945**

1903 • Dr. Thomas D. Clark

1935 • Loretta Lynn

1936 • Martha Layne Collins

1942 • Muhammad Ali

1944 • Phillip A. Sharp

1945 • Diane Sawyer

1952 • Ernie Fletcher

Phillip A. Sharp

1944–
- Molecular biologist
- Won the Nobel Prize in 1993 for his scientific work

Diane Sawyer

1945–
- Famous journalist
- Has been part of many television news programs viewed by millions of people

1936–

- In 1983, became Kentucky's first woman governor
- A former teacher, she worked especially hard for education reform

1942–

- Champion boxer
- Converted to Islam in 1964
- Received the Presidential Medal of Freedom in 2005 for his civil rights work

1966   **1987**   **Present**

2005

1964 • Mary T. Meagher Plant

Ernie Fletcher

Mary T. Meagher Plant

1952–

- Elected governor of Kentucky in 2003
- Served as a fighter pilot in the United States Air Force

1964–

- Record-setting swimmer
- Won three gold medals in the 1984 Olympic Games

Place

Kentucky Today

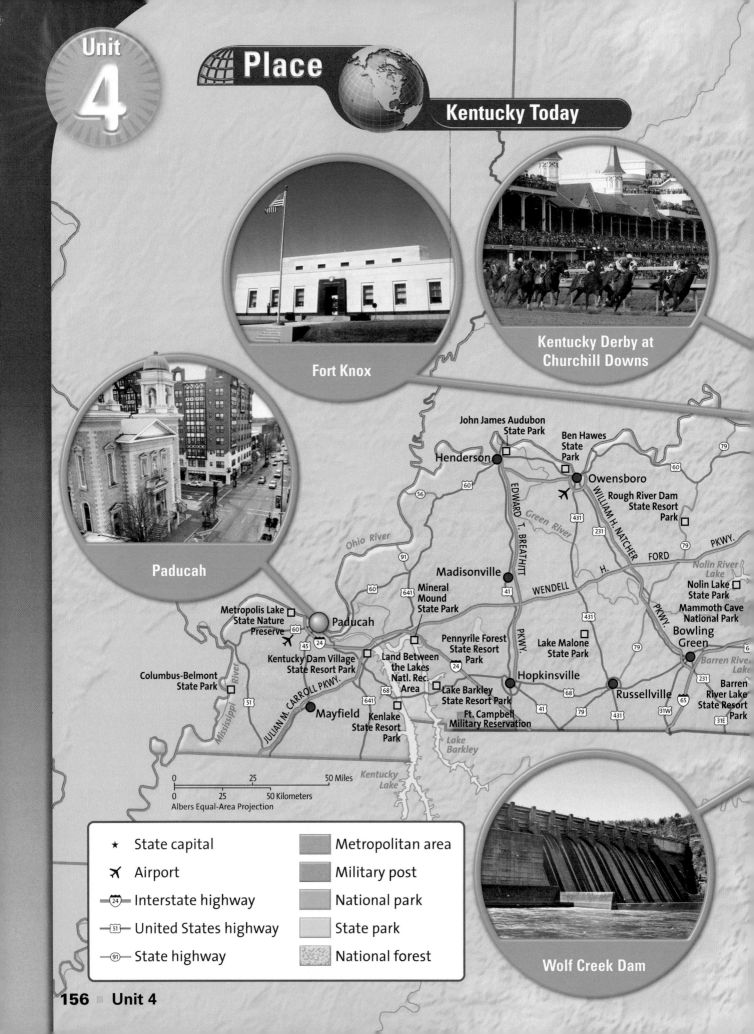

Fort Knox

Kentucky Derby at Churchill Downs

Paducah

John James Audubon State Park

Ben Hawes State Park

Henderson

Owensboro

Rough River Dam State Resort Park

Madisonville

Nolin Lake State Park

Mammoth Cave National Park

Bowling Green

Mineral Mound State Park

Metropolis Lake State Nature Preserve

Paducah

Kentucky Dam Village State Resort Park

Pennyrile Forest State Resort Park

Lake Malone State Park

Land Between the Lakes Natl. Rec. Area

Columbus-Belmont State Park

Hopkinsville

Russellville

Barren River Lake State Resort Park

Lake Barkley State Resort Park

Mayfield

Kenlake State Resort Park

Ft. Campbell Military Reservation

Lake Barkley

Kentucky Lake

0   25   50 Miles
0   25   50 Kilometers
Albers Equal-Area Projection

★ State capital

✈ Airport

24 Interstate highway

51 United States highway

91 State highway

Metropolitan area

Military post

National park

State park

National forest

Wolf Creek Dam

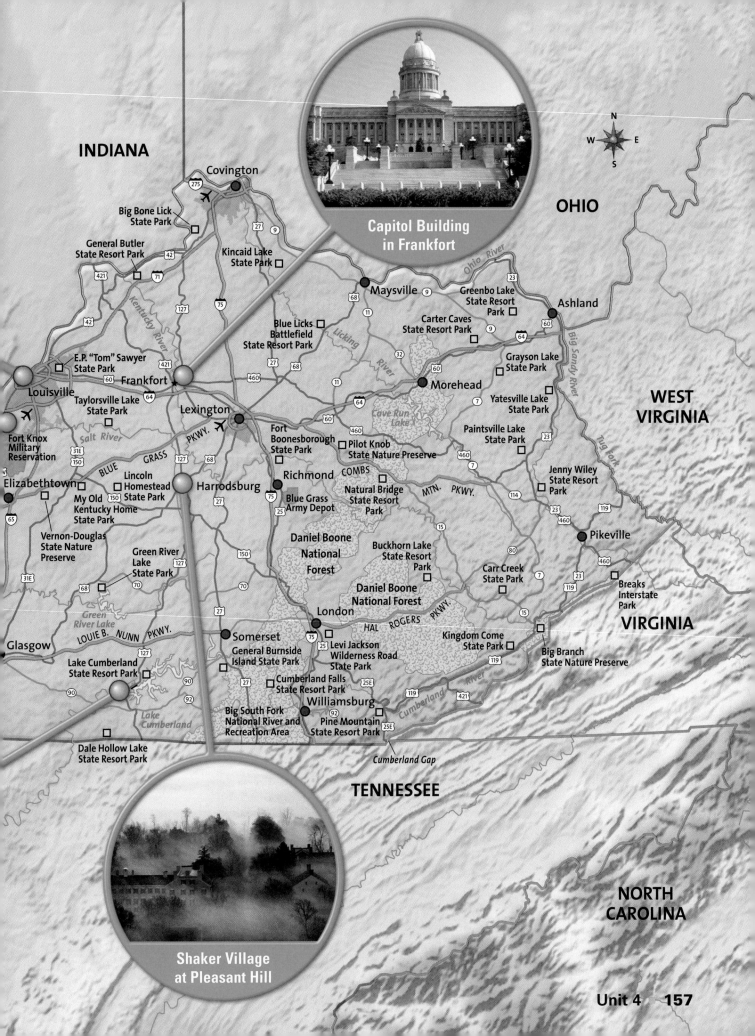

INDIANA

OHIO

Covington

Big Bone Lick
State Park

General Butler
State Resort Park

Kincaid Lake
State Park

**Capitol Building
in Frankfort**

Maysville

Greenbo Lake
State Resort
Park

Ashland

Blue Licks
Battlefield
State Resort Park

Carter Caves
State Resort Park

Grayson Lake
State Park

E.P. "Tom" Sawyer
State Park

Frankfort

Morehead

WEST
VIRGINIA

Louisville

Taylorsville Lake
State Park

Lexington

Cave Run
Lake

Yatesville Lake
State Park

Fort Knox
Military
Reservation

Fort
Boonesborough
State Park

Pilot Knob
State Nature Preserve

Paintsville Lake
State Park

Jenny Wiley
State Resort
Park

BLUE GRASS

Lincoln
Homestead
State Park

Harrodsburg

Richmond

COMBS

Elizabethtown

My Old
Kentucky Home
State Park

Blue Grass
Army Depot

Natural Bridge
State Resort
Park

MTN. PKWY.

Pikeville

Vernon-Douglas
State Nature
Preserve

Daniel Boone

Buckhorn Lake
State Resort
Park

National

Breaks
Interstate
Park

Green River
Lake
State Park

Forest

Carr Creek
State Park

VIRGINIA

Green
River Lake

Daniel Boone
National Forest

Glasgow

London

HAL ROGERS PKWY.

LOUIE B. NUNN PKWY.

Somerset

Kingdom Come
State Park

Big Branch
State Nature Preserve

Lake Cumberland
State Resort Park

General Burnside
Island State Park

Levi Jackson
Wilderness Road
State Park

Cumberland Falls
State Resort Park

Williamsburg

Lake
Cumberland

Big South Fork
National River and
Recreation Area

Pine Mountain
State Resort Park

Cumberland Gap

Dale Hollow Lake
State Resort Park

**Shaker Village
at Pleasant Hill**

TENNESSEE

NORTH
CAROLINA

Kentucky's People Today

COMPARE AND CONTRAST

YOU ARE THERE

You've been looking forward to this day all year, and now it's finally here—the family reunion. Relatives from all over Kentucky and the United States have come to your aunt Kathy's farm to share food and stories and family fun! Your grandfather has just finished telling a story about his childhood on a small farm during the Depression. Now your uncle John picks up a mandolin and starts to sing an old bluegrass song. You wonder what other surprises are in store.

❯ **KENTUCKIANS** Many different people call Kentucky home.

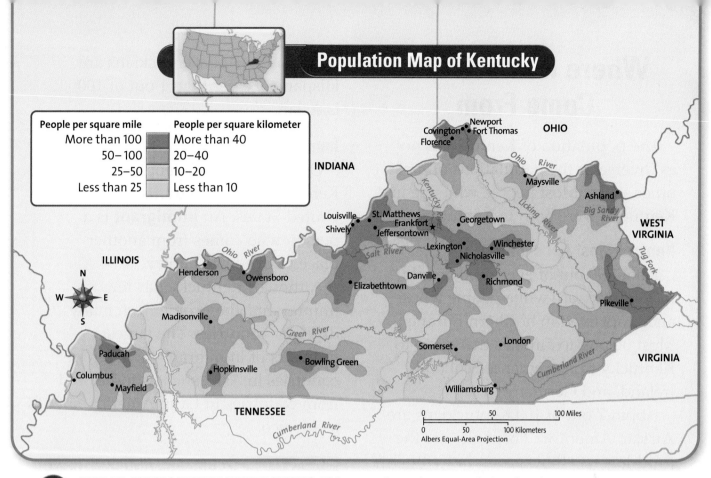

Population Map of Kentucky

People per square mile
More than 100
50–100
25–50
Less than 25

People per square kilometer
More than 40
20–40
10–20
Less than 10

OHIO
Newport
Covington • Fort Thomas
Florence
INDIANA
Ohio River
Maysville
Ashland
Big Sandy River
WEST VIRGINIA
Louisville
St. Matthews
Frankfort ★
Jeffersontown
Georgetown
Shively
Lexington
Winchester
Nicholasville
Tug Fork
ILLINOIS
Salt River
Henderson
Owensboro
Danville
Richmond
Elizabethtown
Pikeville
Madisonville
Green River
VIRGINIA
Somerset
London
Paducah
Bowling Green
Cumberland River
Columbus
Hopkinsville
Mayfield
Williamsburg
TENNESSEE
Cumberland River

0   50   100 Miles
0   50   100 Kilometers
Albers Equal-Area Projection

MAP SKILL **HUMAN-ENVIRONMENT INTERACTIONS** This map shows how population density varies across Kentucky. What is the population density near where you live?

Population

Today, more than 4 million people live in Kentucky. The population of the state is growing, but not as fast as it did at times in the past. From 2000 to 2004, the population grew from about 4,042,000 to about 4,146,000. That's an increase of more than 100,000 people.

People per Square Mile

Kentucky's population is spread over the state's 39,728 square miles of land. That gives Kentucky a population density of about 104 people per square mile. **Population density** is the number of people who live in an area of a certain size.

Where Kentuckians Live

Kentucky's people are not spread evenly around the state. **Jefferson County**, where Louisville is, has about 700,000 people. Its population density is more than 18,000 people per square mile. **Pike County**, where Pikeville is, has about 69,000 people. Its population density is only 87 people per square mile.

Such differences mean that Kentucky has an uneven population distribution. **Population distribution** is how a place's population is spread throughout the place.

READING CHECK ⟡COMPARE AND CONTRAST
How does Jefferson County's population density contrast with Pike County's?

Where Kentuckians Come From

The population of Kentucky is not as diverse as the populations of most other states. Most people who live in Kentucky were born in Kentucky.

Kentuckians' Ancestors

About 90 out of every 100 people in Kentucky are white people whose ancestors lived in northern Europe. Most belong to families that came to Kentucky from England, Scotland, Ireland, and Germany.

About 7 out of 100 Kentuckians are African American. Hispanics are the third-largest ethnic group in Kentucky. An **ethnic group** is a group of people from the same country, or of the same race, or with a shared culture. Fewer than 2 out of 100 Kentuckians are Hispanic. Fewer than 1 out of 100 is Asian.

Immigrants

Only 2 out of 100 people in Kentucky are immigrants to the United States. An **immigrant** is a person who comes from another place to live in a country.

Although Kentucky has few immigrants, they come from many different countries. The largest numbers of immigrants come from countries in Asia, such as India, and from countries in Latin America, such as Mexico.

READING CHECK ⟳ **COMPARE AND CONTRAST**
Is the population of Kentucky more or less diverse than the populations of most other states?

❯ **SHARED CULTURE Many people in Glasgow, Kentucky, celebrate their Scottish heritage.**

▶ QUILTING is an important custom in Kentucky. Many Kentuckians enjoy making quilts (left) and admiring them (above).

Customs

Kentuckians share many customs with Americans who live in other states. They also have customs that set them apart.

Passing It On

Many Kentuckians live their whole lives in the state. They remain close to extended families of grandparents, aunts and uncles, and cousins. This closeness plays an important role in Kentucky customs.

Family reunions are common in Kentucky. People tell stories about family history and eat foods made from recipes handed down from one generation to the next.

Many families pass along much more than recipes. Parents and grandparents teach children skills such as fishing and quilt making. Kentucky is known for its stonemasons, who are expert at using natural stone to build walls and buildings. Stonemasons often pass on this skill to younger family members.

Sometimes, visiting a special place in Kentucky can become a family custom or tradition. **Rosemary Clooney**, a famous singer who grew up in Kentucky, took her grandchildren to see a meadow that was special to her as a child:

> **❝On summer nights, that meadow has fireflies that almost light up the Earth. I've driven my grandchildren there to show them this, and they're filled with as much wonder as I was when I was a child.❞**

READING CHECK **MAIN IDEA AND DETAILS**
What are some of the customs that people in Kentucky share?

Religion in Kentucky

A key part of the heritage of many Kentuckians is their religion. Kentucky is in a part of the United States that is sometimes called the Bible Belt. The **Bible Belt** stretches from Virginia and the Carolinas west to Oklahoma and Texas. In this region, most people are Christians, and religion plays an important role in their lives.

Christian Churches

About 90 percent of Kentuckians who practice a religion are Christians. The largest Christian group in Kentucky is the Southern Baptist Convention with about 980,000 members. The Roman Catholic Church is the second-largest Christian group, with more than 400,000 members. Other Christian churches in Kentucky include Methodist, Christian Church and Church of Christ, African American Baptist, and Church of Christ.

Another Christian group found in Kentucky is the Amish. Amish is the name of the group's Christian religion and its culture. The Amish live a simple way of life without most modern conveniences. Some Amish,

▶ RELIGIONS Three of the religions that Kentuckians practice are the Christian religion (below), the Jewish religion (right), and the Muslim religion (below right).

like those of **Crittenden County**, moved to Kentucky in the late 1970s.

Other Religions

People who belong to other religions also live in Kentucky. The state has more than 11,000 Jewish people and about 4,700 Muslims. Small numbers of Buddhists, Hindus, and members of the Baha'i faith are also part of Kentucky's religious community.

READING CHECK **MAIN IDEA AND DETAILS**
What are some of the different religions people in Kentucky practice?

Summary

More than 4 million people live in Kentucky. Nine out of 10 are white people whose ancestors came from northern Europe. Many Kentuckians stay close to their families and pass traditions and skills on to their children. Most Kentuckians are Christians.

▶ **THE HINDU RELIGION** Some Kentuckians practice the Hindu religion.

REVIEW

1. WHAT TO KNOW What are the people of Kentucky like today?

2. VOCABULARY How is **population density** different from **population distribution**?

3. HISTORY What countries did the ancestors of most Kentuckians come from?

4. CRITICAL THINKING What are the similarities and differences between Kentucky's population today and its population during the time of early settlement?

5. ✏️ **WRITE AN EXPLANATION** Write a paragraph that explains a Kentucky custom, one that you participate in or another.

6. ⭐Focus Skill **COMPARE AND CONTRAST** On a separate sheet of paper, copy and complete the graphic organizer below.

Topic 1
Most state populations are very diverse.

Similar

Topic 2
Kentucky's population is not as diverse as that of most states.

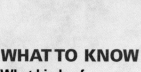

Education, Arts, and Culture

WHAT TO KNOW
What kinds of writing, music, art, and entertainment are part of Kentucky's culture?

VOCABULARY
craft p. 167

PEOPLE
Phillip A. Sharp
William Wells Brown
Robert Penn Warren
Bobbie Ann Mason
Barbara Kingsolver
Diane Sawyer
Loretta Lynn
John James Audubon
Henry Lawrence Faulkner
Mary T. Meagher Plant

PLACES
Guthrie
Mayfield
Glasgow
Louisville
Johnson County
Simpson County

COMPARE AND CONTRAST

YOU ARE THERE
You and your classmates are watching a film about Kentucky's history and its people. Instead of viewing it on a television or movie screen, you are watching it on the Internet. You like how the movie is helping bring history to life. You also are enjoying learning about people who live in other regions of Kentucky.

This is just one way students in your school learn about the world around them. Going to school provides you with an opportunity for a bright future.

> **INTERNET ACCESS** Almost every school in Kentucky provides Internet access to its students.

> TRANSYLVANIA UNIVERSITY Students walk across the campus at Kentucky's oldest college.

Education

Kentucky's first schools opened when early settlement began. Today, state law requires all children between the ages of 6 and 16 to attend school.

Public Schools

The state set up a public school system in 1849. At that time, some parents did not want to send their children to school. They needed the children to help with farmwork. Over time, however, more and more Kentucky children attended school.

At present, Kentucky's public schools lead the nation in some areas. The percentage of students who attend college is rising faster in Kentucky than in any other state. Students' scores on achievement tests are rising, too. One famous former student who attended Kentucky's public schools is **Phillip A. Sharp**, who won a Nobel Prize in 1993 for his work in science.

Colleges

Transylvania University was Kentucky's first college. It was founded in 1780 and is located in Lexington. Today, the state has more than 30 colleges and universities. Almost a quarter of a million students are enrolled in Kentucky's universities.

READING CHECK ☼**COMPARE AND CONTRAST**
How has attendance in Kentucky's public schools changed since 1849?

Writers

Many Kentucky writers have found success and fame. Nearly all of them have written about the state and its people in some of their books, stories, and poems.

An Early Writer

William Wells Brown was born as an enslaved person near Lexington. He escaped to the North in 1834. Brown later wrote *The Narrative of William Wells Brown, a Fugitive Slave, Written by Himself*. Other books followed. Brown was one of the first African Americans to write a novel, a play, and a travel book.

Literature and Journalism

Robert Penn Warren was born in **Guthrie** in 1905. He wrote novels, stories, and poems. Warren won three Pulitzer Prizes and many other awards. He was the first Poet Laureate, or official poet, of the United States.

Bobbie Ann Mason was born in **Mayfield**. Many of her novels and stories are set in rural areas of western Kentucky.

Barbara Kingsolver was born in Maryland but moved to Kentucky with her family when she was two years old. Her best-known novels concern the strengths of poor people.

Diane Sawyer is one of the best-known television journalists in the country. She was born in **Glasgow**, Kentucky, and grew up in **Louisville**.

READING CHECK ☼**MAIN IDEA AND DETAILS**
What kinds of writing is William Wells Brown known for?

> **KENTUCKY WRITERS** Some well-known Kentucky writers are—from left to right— Barbara Kingsolver, William Wells Brown, Robert Penn Warren, and Bobbie Ann Mason.

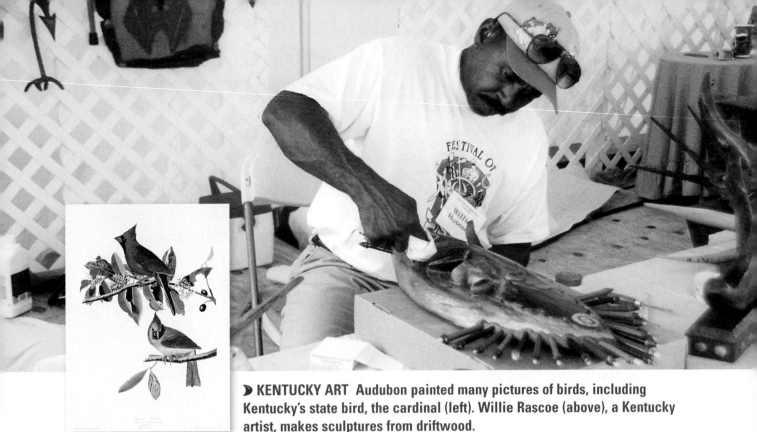

▶ KENTUCKY ART Audubon painted many pictures of birds, including Kentucky's state bird, the cardinal (left). Willie Rascoe (above), a Kentucky artist, makes sculptures from driftwood.

Music and Art

Kentucky has produced famous musicians and artists, too. In addition, many Kentucky craftworkers, though not widely known, are artists in their own right.

Bluegrass and Country Music

Bluegrass is Kentucky's best-known music. It is not the only music that has made Kentucky singers famous, however.

Country singer **Loretta Lynn** became known throughout the nation for her song "Coal Miner's Daughter." She grew up in **Johnson County**. In 1972, she was the first woman to be named the Country Music Association's entertainer of the year. In 1980, Loretta Lynn was named entertainer of the decade.

Artists

John James Audubon arrived in Louisville in 1807. He began painting pictures of the area's birds. Over time, he made accurate pictures of hundreds of birds. The paintings were published in four books between 1827 and 1838. These books, known as *Birds of America*, are still admired today.

Henry Lawrence Faulkner, from **Simpson County**, lived in the 1900s. He is known for his paintings of Kentucky landscapes and animals.

Craftworkers

Kentucky is well-known for its crafts. A **craft** is a special skill used to make useful objects. Kentucky craftworkers make quilts, furniture, baskets, and many other objects.

READING CHECK MAIN IDEA AND DETAILS
What is Henry Lawrence Faulkner known for?

Kentucky Fun

Kentuckians enjoy watching sporting events and taking part in the state's many festivals. Some events draw visitors from around the world.

Sports

The Kentucky Derby is one of the nation's oldest horse races. It is also one of the most famous. Each year, on the first Saturday in May, thousands gather in Louisville to watch the race.

Many Kentuckians are fans of college basketball. The University of Kentucky men's basketball team has won seven national championships.

Kentuckians have also taken part in the Olympic Games. **Mary T. Meagher**

Plant, from Louisville, won three gold medals for swimming in 1984.

Festivals

The people of Kentucky celebrate their past and present at yearly festivals. These festivals focus on everything from Kentucky music and crafts to Scottish games.

At Lexington's Dulcimer Festival, people gather to play and listen to this regional instrument. The Scottish Highland Games, held in Glasgow, Kentucky, feature Scottish music, dancing, and sports contests. The Corn Island Storytelling Festival in Louisville entertains those who enjoy hearing Kentucky tales. These are just a few of the state's many festivals.

▶ **THE KENTUCKY DERBY** is one of the nation's oldest and most well-known horse races.

countries. In fact, the state's exports doubled between 1996 and 2004.

Kentucky exports more livestock and horses than any other state. However, most of the state's exports are manufactured goods. They include cars, trucks, and chemicals.

Kentucky's main trading partners are Canada, Mexico, the countries of western Europe, China, and Japan.

READING CHECK **MAIN IDEA AND DETAILS**
How is Kentucky's economy connected to the world?

Summary

Kentucky has a market economy. Service industries make up the biggest part of the state's economy. Manufacturing industries, mining, and agriculture also play important roles. Imports and exports connect Kentucky to countries around the world.

▶ **DISTRIBUTION** These barges on the Ohio River at Louisville help distribute Kentucky's products to other places.

REVIEW

1. **WHAT TO KNOW** What are the main parts of Kentucky's economy today?

2. **VOCABULARY** How do **service industries** differ from manufacturing industries?

3. **ECONOMICS** What is Kentucky's largest manufacturing industry?

4. **CRITICAL THINKING** Why do you think most of Kentucky's manufacturing industries are in and around the state's largest cities?

5. **WRITE A JOB DESCRIPTION** Choose a job that you would like to have when you are an adult. Write a paragraph describing the job.

6. **COMPARE AND CONTRAST** On a separate sheet of paper, copy and complete the graphic organizer below.

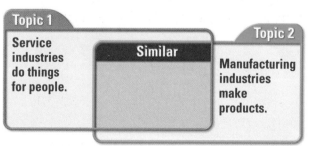

Topic 1
Service industries do things for people.

Similar

Topic 2
Manufacturing industries make products.

Make Economic Choices

Why It Matters When you make decisions about what to buy, you are making economic choices.

❱ LEARN

Sometimes you want to buy two items but have enough money for only one. If you give up one thing to buy another, you make a **trade-off**. What you do not buy becomes the **opportunity cost**. Follow these steps to make good economic choices.

Step 1 List the things that you would like to buy and how much each one costs.

Step 2 Decide how much money you have and how much you want to spend and save.

Step 3 Decide what you can buy with the money. Think about the trade-offs and opportunity costs.

Step 4 Make an economic choice. Then think about why your decision was the best choice.

❱ **GOVERNMENT CHOICES** The government in Kentucky makes economic choices when it decides how to use the tax money it collects. These workers are being paid by the government to repair a bridge in Lexington.

▶ **PEOPLE MAKE CHOICES** Every day, people make economic choices. This girl is choosing to spend money on groceries instead of buying something else.

▶ PRACTICE

Imagine that your class is visiting a natural history museum. At the museum gift store, you want to buy a T-shirt, which costs $12. You also want to buy a DVD about prehistoric animals. It costs $14. You have $15 to spend. Use the steps below to make your economic choice.

1 What do you want to buy, and how much does each item cost?

2 How much money do you have to spend?

3 What is the trade-off and the opportunity cost of each economic choice? Which item do you want more?

4 Make your choice.

▶ APPLY

Think of two products or services that you would like to buy. Suppose that you have enough money to buy one item, but not both. Explain to a partner the trade-off and the opportunity cost of each choice. Then tell which economic choice you would make, and why.

Citizenship Skills

Kentucky State Government

WHAT TO KNOW
How is Kentucky's state government organized?

VOCABULARY
amendment p. 181
legislative branch p. 182
executive branch p. 182
judicial branch p. 183
political system p. 184

PEOPLE
Ernie Fletcher

PLACES
Frankfort

COMPARE AND CONTRAST
Focus Skill

YOU ARE THERE

You are visiting the state capitol building in **Frankfort**. You listen as state representatives talk about a proposed law. Some of the representatives are in favor of the law, but some are against it. They give speeches, hoping to persuade others to agree with their side. Finally, the representatives begin to cast their votes. You are watching state government in action!

The House of Representatives chamber

First Steps

Kentucky's official name is the Commonwealth of Kentucky. The word *commonwealth* means "for the good of everyone."

A Commonwealth

Kentucky is one of only four states to have the word *commonwealth* in its name. The others are Virginia, Pennsylvania, and Massachusetts. In spite of this unusual name, Kentucky's state government is very much like the governments of the other 49 states.

A Constitution

Kentucky's state government began with its constitution.

Kentucky's first constitution was written in 1792. Later, in 1799, the state improved its constitution.

Kentuckians changed their constitution two more times, in 1850 and in 1891. The 1891 constitution is still in use today.

The current constitution is not exactly the same as it was in 1891, however. The state has made some changes to it over the years. Kentucky voters have approved all of these changes, also called **amendments**. These changes have helped bring the constitution up to date.

READING CHECK ☼ **COMPARE AND CONTRAST**
What does Kentucky have in common with Virginia?

The capitol dome

The State Capitol

ILLUSTRATION The construction of the Kentucky state capitol building was completed in 1910. Which branch of the state government are the House of Representatives and the Senate a part of?

The Senate chamber

A statue of Abraham Lincoln

Branches of Government

Kentucky's constitution set up three branches of state government. They are the legislative branch, the executive branch, and the judicial branch. The constitution explains what each branch does.

The Legislative Branch

The **legislative branch** makes state laws. The Kentucky legislature is called the General Assembly. It has two parts, the House of Representatives and the Senate. The House of Representatives has 100 members. The Senate has 38 members.

The General Assembly meets in the state's capital city, Frankfort. It normally meets every year for a session that lasts 60 days.

The Executive Branch

The **executive branch** enforces, or carries out, state laws. The executive branch also makes the state budget. A budget is a plan for spending money.

The governor is the leader of the state's executive branch. He or she has many duties. The governor appoints

FAST FACT

The governor's mansion in Frankfort was completed in 1914. It is one of the few governor's mansions in the country that offers tours to the public.

people to many jobs in the state government.

Kentuckians elect a governor every four years. Governors are allowed to serve a second term if the voters wish. To run for governor, a person must be at least 30 years old. He or she also must have lived in Kentucky for at least six years. **Ernie Fletcher** was elected governor of Kentucky in 2003.

The Judicial Branch

The **judicial branch** is made up of the state courts. Kentucky's judicial branch has four levels of courts. These courts make sure that state laws agree with the Kentucky constitution. State courts also make sure that the laws are carried out fairly.

Kentucky's Model

Kentucky's state government borrows many ideas from the United States government. Dividing the government into three branches is one of those ideas. This division keeps any one person or group from having too much power. Each branch limits the power of the other two.

READING CHECK ○COMPARE AND CONTRAST
How does Kentucky's state government compare to the United States government?

TABLE No branch of the state government is more powerful than another. **What are the duties of the legislative branch?**

Branches of Kentucky's State Government

LEGISLATIVE BRANCH	EXECUTIVE BRANCH	JUDICIAL BRANCH
Proposes bills and makes state laws	Enforces state laws, or sees that they are carried out	Decides whether state laws have been broken or whether they go against the state constitution

The Federal System

Like all states, Kentucky takes part in this country's federal system of government. A federal system is one kind of **political system**, or system of government. In a federal system, the national government and the state governments each have certain powers.

Powers of the National Government

The national government has power over matters that affect all Americans. It is more powerful than any state government.

Only the national government has the power to declare war and to make peace. The national government also has the power to print money and to control trade among the states. The power to make laws about citizenship and immigration belongs to the national government, too. Finally, only the national government can create an army and a navy.

Powers of the State Governments

Only state governments have the power to control trade within the state. State governments also set up local governments and public schools.

TABLE The powers given to federal, state, and local governments help them maintain order, protect the rights of individuals, and promote the common good. Why do you think each level of government has the power to collect taxes?

Federal System of Government

SOME POWERS OF THE FEDERAL GOVERNMENT

- Control trade between states and with foreign countries
- Create and maintain an army and a navy
- Print and coin money
- Admit new states
- Make laws for immigration and citizenship
- Declare war and make peace

SHARED POWERS

- Collect taxes
- Set up court systems
- Borrow money
- Make laws to provide for public health and welfare
- Make sure laws are obeyed

SOME POWERS OF THE STATE GOVERNMENT

- Set up public schools
- Set up local governments
- Conduct elections
- Control trade within the state
- Make laws for marriage and divorce
- Set qualifications for voting

SOME POWERS OF THE LOCAL GOVERNMENT

- Set up local services such as fire protection and waterworks
- Set up local libraries and parks

▶ KENTUCKY NATIONAL GUARD These family members work for the Kentucky National Guard.

State governments cannot create armies, but states do have other kinds of military forces. The Kentucky National Guard is one of the oldest military groups in the United States. The governor of Kentucky is its commander in chief.

Shared Powers

The national government and the state governments share some powers. Both the national government and the state governments can set up court systems. Both also have the power to collect taxes.

READING CHECK **MAIN IDEA AND DETAILS**
What are some of the powers of Kentucky's state government?

Summary

Kentucky's state constitution organizes the state government into three branches. They are the legislative branch, the executive branch, and the judicial branch. Kentucky plays a role in the nation's federal system of government.

REVIEW

1. **WHAT TO KNOW** How is Kentucky's state government organized?

2. **VOCABULARY** How are the duties of the **legislative branch** different from those of the **executive branch**?

3. **GOVERNMENT** Who is the leader of the executive branch of Kentucky's state government?

4. **CRITICAL THINKING** Why do you think the federal and state governments are divided into three branches?

5. **WRITE A LETTER TO THE EDITOR** Write a letter to the editor of a newspaper in your community. Describe a new law that you would like the General Assembly to pass. Give at least one reason why people should support the law.

6. **COMPARE AND CONTRAST** On a (Focus Skill) separate sheet of paper, copy and complete the graphic organizer below.

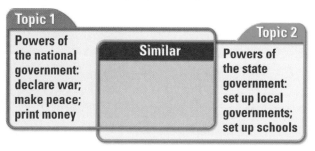

Topic 1
Powers of the national government: declare war; make peace; print money

Similar

Topic 2
Powers of the state government: set up local governments; set up schools

Local Governments

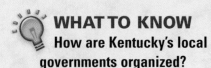
VOCABULARY
county p. 187
county seat p. 188
magistrate p. 188
municipal p. 189
commission p. 189

PEOPLE
Colonel William Oldham
Isaac Shelby
Robert Trimble

PLACES
La Grange
Oldham County
Shelby County
Trimble County
Frankfort
Bowling Green
Fayette County
Lexington
Jefferson County
Louisville

 **COMPARE AND CONTRAST**

YOU ARE THERE Today your class is visiting the courthouse in **La Grange**, where you have lived all your life. You have ridden your bike by the courthouse a thousand times. Until today, though, you did not know that the courthouse was the workplace of all who help govern **Oldham County**. You also learned that Oldham County was named after **Colonel William Oldham**, who fought in the American Revolution.

❯ OLDHAM COUNTY COURTHOUSE

▶ **FIREFIGHTERS** work to put out a fire in Nicholasville, Kentucky.

Local Governments

Local governments take care of matters that affect people in specific communities. Local governments build and repair roads. They provide schools, libraries, and parks. They maintain police departments and fire departments. In many places, local governments provide public utilities such as water, electricity, and trash collection.

Kentucky Counties

Kentucky has two main kinds of local governments. They are city governments and county governments.

A **county** is a section of a state. Kentucky is divided into 120 counties. Only two states, Texas and Georgia, have more counties than Kentucky.

Many Kentucky counties were set up during the 1800s. Some are named after famous Kentuckians. **Shelby County** was named after **Isaac Shelby**, the state's first governor. **Trimble County** was named after **Robert Trimble**. He was a Kentucky lawyer who became a United States Supreme Court justice.

READING CHECK ŎCOMPARE AND CONTRAST
How does the number of counties in Kentucky compare with that in other states?

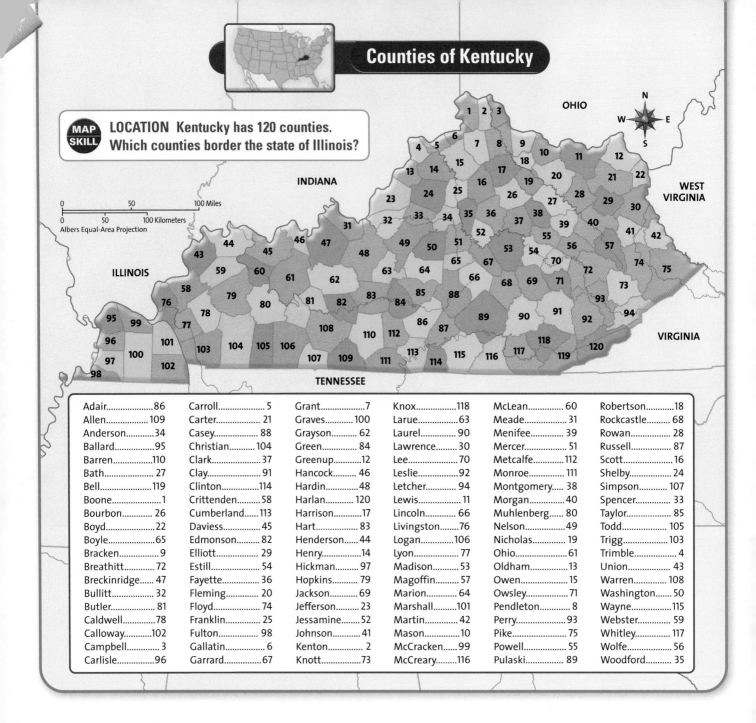

Counties of Kentucky

MAP SKILL LOCATION Kentucky has 120 counties. Which counties border the state of Illinois?

Adair..............86	Carroll..............5	Grant..............7	Knox..............118	McLean..............60	Robertson..............18
Allen..............109	Carter..............21	Graves..........100	Larue..............63	Meade..............31	Rockcastle..........68
Anderson..........34	Casey..............88	Grayson..........62	Laurel..............90	Menifee..............39	Rowan..............28
Ballard..........95	Christian..........104	Green..............84	Lawrence..........30	Mercer..............51	Russell..............87
Barren..........110	Clark..............37	Greenup..........12	Lee..............70	Metcalfe..........112	Scott..............16
Bath..............27	Clay..............91	Hancock..........46	Leslie..............92	Monroe..............111	Shelby..............24
Bell..............119	Clinton..........114	Hardin..............48	Letcher..............94	Montgomery.....38	Simpson..........107
Boone..............1	Crittenden..........58	Harlan..........120	Lewis..............11	Morgan..............40	Spencer..............33
Bourbon..........26	Cumberland......113	Harrison..........17	Lincoln..............66	Muhlenberg......80	Taylor..............85
Boyd..............22	Daviess..........45	Hart..............83	Livingston.......76	Nelson..............49	Todd..............105
Boyle..............65	Edmonson..........82	Henderson......44	Logan..............106	Nicholas..............19	Trigg..............103
Bracken..........9	Elliott..............29	Henry..............14	Lyon..............77	Ohio..............61	Trimble..............4
Breathitt..........72	Estill..............54	Hickman..........97	Madison..........53	Oldham..............13	Union..............43
Breckinridge......47	Fayette..............36	Hopkins..........79	Magoffin..........57	Owen..............15	Warren..............108
Bullitt..............32	Fleming..............20	Jackson..........69	Marion..............64	Owsley..............71	Washington.........50
Butler..............81	Floyd..............74	Jefferson..........23	Marshall..........101	Pendleton..........8	Wayne..............115
Caldwell..........78	Franklin..........25	Jessamine........52	Martin..............42	Perry..............93	Webster..............59
Calloway..........102	Fulton..............98	Johnson..........41	Mason..............10	Pike..............75	Whitley..............117
Campbell..........3	Gallatin..............6	Kenton..............2	McCracken.....99	Powell..............55	Wolfe..............56
Carlisle..............96	Garrard..............67	Knott..............73	McCreary.........116	Pulaski..............89	Woodford..........35

County and City Governments

Each Kentucky county has a county seat. The **county seat** is the town or city where the county government is located. In Kentucky, the leader of the county government is the county judge executive. Voters in the county elect this person.

County Workers

Voters also elect people who help the county judge executive. These elected helpers are sometimes called **magistrates**. Most counties have more than one magistrate.

Counties also have other workers. They often include a sheriff, who enforces the laws. A county clerk keeps records about important events in the county, such as marriages and the buying and selling of land.

A county may also have a treasurer, who is responsible for its money. Some counties have fire departments, parks departments, and animal shelters.

City Governments

Today, Kentucky has hundreds of towns and cities. Each one has its own government. These city governments are known as **municipal** governments.

Kentucky cities have different forms of government. Some cities, including **Frankfort** and **Bowling Green**, have commission-manager governments. A **commission** is a group of people who are chosen to run a government.

A commission-manager government has two parts, a city commission and a city manager. The commissioners work together to make laws and decisions for the city. The city manager handles the city's day-to-day business.

Other Kentucky cities are governed by a commission but have no city manager. Still others have a mayor and a council. A council's duties are similar to those of a commission. Finally, some cities are governed by a mayor and a group of aldermen. An alderman is similar to a city council member or a city commissioner.

READING CHECK SUMMARIZE
What services do county governments provide?

▶ GOVERNMENT SERVICES Trash collection and snow plowing services are provided by county or city governments.

Other Local Governments

A few Kentucky cities and counties have combined their governments to create new forms of local government.

New Kinds of Government

In 1974, **Fayette County** and the city of **Lexington** combined their governments to create a single local government. The Lexington-Fayette Urban County Government has a mayor and an urban council. Both the mayor and the council are elected by voters.

The purposes of this change were to save money and to provide better services. Because Lexington was the only city in Fayette County, the city and county governments were serving the same people. They were providing many of the same services.

In 2003, **Jefferson County** and the city of **Louisville** also combined their governments. Their new, combined government is called Louisville Metro.

Louisville Metro is different from the Lexington-Fayette Urban County Government. Jefferson County has other cities besides Louisville. Those other cities are part of the Louisville Metro government. However, they continue to also have their own city governments.

▶ **THE LEXINGTON-FAYETTE URBAN COUNTY GOVERNMENT** serves the people of Lexington and of Fayette County. Above is the government's seal.

▶ **THE OLD LOUISVILLE NATIONAL HISTORIC PRESERVATION DISTRICT** is a special district that helps preserve Kentucky's rich history.

Special Districts

Cities and counties are often divided into even smaller areas, or districts. Special districts are created to provide a specific service. School districts and voting districts are special districts.

READING CHECK ⏺**COMPARE AND CONTRAST**
How is the Louisville Metro different from the Lexington-Fayette Urban County Government?

Summary

Kentucky has two main kinds of local governments—county governments and city governments. A few counties and cities have combined their governments to create new kinds of local governments. In addition, most cities and counties have special districts.

REVIEW

1. **WHAT TO KNOW** How are Kentucky's local governments organized?

2. **VOCABULARY** What role does a **county seat** play in local government?

3. **GOVERNMENT** Describe one new kind of local government in Kentucky.

4. **CRITICAL THINKING** What might be an advantage of having fewer counties?

5. ✎ **WRITE A CAMPAIGN BROCHURE** Imagine that you are trying to be elected as the leader of a local government in Kentucky. Write a campaign brochure telling why people should vote for you.

6. (Focus Skill) **COMPARE AND CONTRAST** On a separate sheet of paper, copy and complete the graphic organizer below.

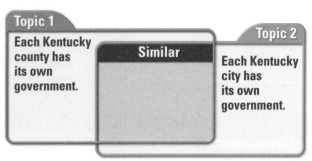

Topic 1
Each Kentucky county has its own government.

Similar

Topic 2
Each Kentucky city has its own government.

Kentucky Citizenship

VOCABULARY

jury trial p. 193
responsibility p. 194
register p. 195
volunteer p. 195

COMPARE AND CONTRAST

YOU ARE THERE
Today is election day. You love going to the polls, the places where people vote, with your parents. Everyone seems excited and happy. That's easy to understand. They are choosing the people who will lead the government. You can't wait until you, too, are old enough to vote!

▶ **VOTING** These voters wait their turn in the Douglas Park section of Lexington.

Kentuckians' Rights

Like the United States government, Kentucky's state government is a democracy. In a democracy, citizens have many rights.

The Freedom to Choose

Kentucky citizens have the right to make choices about their lives. As stated in the Bill of Rights in the Kentucky Constitution, they have the right of "seeking and pursuing their safety and happiness."

Kentuckians also have the right to follow the religion of their choice or to have no religion. They have the right to express their ideas and opinions. They have the right to assemble, or meet together, and share their opinions with others. Kentucky citizens also have the right to a free press.

The right to own and protect property is another important right. It means that people can own homes, businesses, farms, and other kinds of property.

Kentuckians also have the right to a **jury trial**. This is a trial in which a group of citizens decides whether a person accused of a crime should be found guilty or not guilty.

Another right that Kentucky citizens enjoy is the right to vote in free elections. This right lets Kentuckians choose their leaders.

READING CHECK ⊙**COMPARE AND CONTRAST**
How are the United States government and Kentucky's state government alike?

Kentuckians' Responsibilities

Kentuckians' rights come with **responsibilities**, or duties. Laws require citizens to carry out certain responsibilities. Other responsibilities are not required by law but are still important.

Required by Law

Kentuckians are required to obey the laws of the nation, of Kentucky, and of their local governments. Governments have the authority to punish people who break laws.

Laws also require Kentucky citizens to pay taxes. A tax is money that a government collects from its citizens. Governments often use tax money to pay for services for citizens. Tax money is also used to pay government workers and to pay for government equipment.

The national government, the state governments, and local governments all have the power to tax citizens. Kentucky has a state sales tax and a state income tax. Kentuckians pay sales tax when they buy certain items in Kentucky. Most Kentuckians who earn money at a job pay a tax on this income.

Kentuckians also must serve on a jury when they are called to do so. Only people who are 18 years of age or older serve on juries.

READING CHECK **SUMMARIZE**
What are some responsibilities that are required by law?

▶ **JURY DUTY** These citizens are being sworn in to serve on a jury.

▶ **VOLUNTEERS** Kentuckians can volunteer to do many useful things, such as assisting an elderly person with a quilting project or helping build homes for the poor.

Taking Part

Serving on a jury is only one way in which citizens take part in government. Citizens have a responsibility to take part in government in other ways, too. Most of these are not required by law. They are things that good citizens do by choice.

Voting

Citizens in a democracy choose their leaders by voting. United States citizens in all 50 states may vote when they reach the age of 18.

In Kentucky, a person must also have lived in the state for at least 28 days before he or she can register to vote. To **register** means to sign up in advance. Registered voters in Kentucky can vote in local, state, and national elections.

Other Responsibilities

Citizens have a responsibility to learn about their country, their state, and their community. This knowledge allows them to make wise choices when they vote. Citizens also have a responsibility to treat other people fairly and to respect their rights.

People have a responsibility to help solve problems in their communities. Many citizens help out as volunteers. A **volunteer** is a person who does something useful without being paid for it. Volunteers may clean up litter or help out after natural disasters.

READING CHECK **SUMMARIZE**
What are Kentucky's requirements to vote?

Protecting the Environment

Citizens of Kentucky also have a duty to protect the state's environment. The environment consists of the surroundings in which people, plants, and animals live.

Using Resources Wisely

Kentuckians depend on natural resources for products and for jobs. In addition, Kentucky's mountains, forests, rivers, and lakes provide enjoyment for people who live there and for visitors.

When people use natural resources, they change the environment. They cut down trees, change the flow of rivers, dig mines, and so on. Often these changes damage the environment. People have a responsibility to use resources in a way that causes as little damage as possible. They need to repair damage that cannot be avoided.

In addition, many resources are scarce. Kentuckians have realized that they need to conserve natural resources. To conserve resources is to protect them and use them wisely.

One way in which Kentuckians conserve resources is by recycling, or using them again. For example, some of the resources in paper products, such as newspapers and magazines, can be recycled to make new products. Recycling tires and some kinds of plastic saves oil. Recycling metal cans and glass bottles also saves mineral resources.

❯ CLEANING UP These volunteers are helping to take the trash out of a sinkhole that was being used as a garbage dump near Mammoth Cave National Park.

People can also use less oil by making use of other sources of energy. Energy from the sun, from the wind, and from water can be used to produce electricity. Sunlight and wind are not limited resources, as oil is.

READING CHECK **MAIN IDEA AND DETAILS**
How do Kentuckians conserve resources?

▶ **THE WOLF CREEK DAM** on Lake Cumberland uses water power to produce electricity.

Summary

As citizens of a democracy, Kentuckians have many rights and responsibilities. They have the right to make choices about their lives. They have a responsibility to take part in government and in their communities. They also have a responsibility to protect the environment.

REVIEW

1. **WHAT TO KNOW** What rights and responsibilities do Kentucky citizens have?

2. **VOCABULARY** Write a sentence that uses the word **responsibility** correctly.

3. **CIVICS AND GOVERNMENT** Why do governments collect taxes from citizens?

4. **CRITICAL THINKING** What do you think is the purpose of having rules and laws? How do the rules at your school compare to the laws of Kentucky?

5. **MAKE A POSTER** Make a poster that encourages people to conserve Kentucky's natural resources.

6. **COMPARE AND CONTRAST** On a separate sheet of paper, copy and complete the graphic organizer below.

Topic 1	Similar	Topic 2
Rights: individual choice, religious freedom, free speech, jury trial		Responsibilities: obey laws, pay taxes, serve on a jury

Symbols of Kentucky

Background Symbols are objects or images that represent something else. The symbols on these pages remind people about what it means to come from Kentucky, and why Kentuckians should be proud.

DBQ **Document-Based Question** Study these primary sources and answer the questions.

STATUE OF ABRAHAM LINCOLN

This statue sits in Hodgenville, Kentucky—the town of Lincoln's birth.

DBQ ❶ Why do you think Kentuckians are proud of Abraham Lincoln?

KENTUCKY QUARTER

The coin shows a Thoroughbred horse and the year Kentucky became a state.

DBQ ❷ Why are coins good places to put state symbols?

THE STATE FLAG AND THE GREAT SEAL OF KENTUCKY

The seal shows two people shaking hands. One is dressed like a pioneer and the other is wearing formal clothing. It also contains the state motto: "United We Stand, Divided We Fall."

DBQ ③ How do the two people connect with the state motto?

KENTUCKY DERBY TROPHY

This trophy is awarded to the winner of the Kentucky Derby.

DBQ ⑤ Why might this be a symbol of Kentucky?

KENTUCKY'S STATE SONG

The state song of Kentucky is called "My Old Kentucky Home."

DBQ ④ What are some reasons Kentuckians might like to have a song about their state?

WRITE ABOUT IT

How do these symbols make you feel about being from Kentucky? Write a paragraph to tell how you feel about them.

GO ONLINE For more resources, go to www.harcourtschool.com/ss1

Review and Test Prep

THE BIG IDEA

Culture and Government Kentuckians are proud of their culture, social institutions, and form of government.

Reading Comprehension and Vocabulary

Kentucky Today

More than 4 million people live in Kentucky. About 90 out of 100 are white people whose ancestors lived in northern Europe. Other Kentuckians have African American, Hispanic, and Asian backgrounds.

Kentucky has been home to many successful writers, artists, and musicians. The state is also famous for the Kentucky Derby horse race.

Service industries make up the biggest part of Kentucky's economy. Manufacturing, mining, and agriculture also play important roles. Imports and exports link Kentucky to the world.

Kentucky's constitution created three branches of state government. They are the legislative branch, the executive branch, and the judicial branch. Under the federal system, Kentucky's state government and the United States government each have certain powers. City governments and county governments are the main kinds of local government.

Citizens of Kentucky have many rights and responsibilities. Voting is both a right and a responsibility.

Read the summary above. Then answer the questions that follow.

1. What are imports?
   A changes
   B goods from other countries
   C special skills used to make useful objects
   D people who come from another place to live in a country

2. What is the population of Kentucky?
   A about 3 million
   B more than 4 million
   C more than 90 million
   D about 100 million

3. What is responsibility?
   A a duty
   B a section of a state
   C a person who is elected to help a county judge
   D a person who does something useful without being paid for it

4. What is the Kentucky Derby?
   A a famous horse race
   B a well-known cattle ranch
   C a soccer team
   D a kind of hat

Facts and Main Ideas

Answer these questions.

5. According to Kentucky state law, who must go to school?

6. What is a mandolin?

7. What is Kentucky's biggest crop?

8. What are the two parts of Kentucky's General Assembly?

9. What are three services that local governments provide?

10. What are two kinds of state taxes that Kentucky has?

Write the letter of the best choice.

11. What is the second-largest ethnic group in Kentucky?
    A Muslims
    B Buddhists
    C Asian Americans
    D African Americans

12. What is John James Audubon known for?
    A country music
    B paintings of birds
    C handmade furniture
    D poems about Kentucky

13. Which of the following is a service industry?
    A mining
    B tourism
    C farming
    D chemicals

14. Which of the following is a power of the Kentucky state government?
    A to print money
    B to declare war
    C to create an army
    D to create a school system

 Critical Thinking

15. Describe a time when people might have to make careful economic choices because of limited resources.

 Skills

Make Economic Choices

Follow the steps on page 178 to complete this exercise.

16. Suppose you wish to buy three different items, but only have enough money to buy two. Write a paragraph describing how you reach your economic choice.

OPEN-RESPONSE

Writing Task 1

Situation: You and your class went on a field trip to a park that was once a strip mine.

Writing Task: Learn more about efforts to reclaim areas that were once strip mines. Then write a paragraph that explains how reclaiming land helps Kentucky's environment.

Writing Task 2

Situation: Your class is taking a trip to Frankfort to meet with some members of Kentucky's state government.

Writing Task: Prepare a question to ask someone from each branch of government about his or her job. Then provide answers to those questions yourself, using what you have learned about the functions of state government.

 For more resources, go to
www.harcourtschool.com/ss1

Fun with Social Studies

Museum Muddle

Can you make six matches?

Bluegrass Music

Tourist Attraction

Providing Fuel for Making Electricity

Center of Kentucky's Government

Kentucky Crafts

Kentucky's Biggest Agricultural Product

A case of the Hidden words

Each picture's name is hiding in one of the answers. Can you find them all? Here is the first one:

abc VOCABULARY

You do this when you buy something hoping it will increase in value.

This word means "duties."

Its a section of a state.

These are special skills used to make useful objects.

This is the surroundings in which we live.

1, 2, 3, 4...

What's another word for city government?
municiPAL government

For Your Reference

ATLAS

ALMANAC

BIOGRAPHICAL DICTIONARY

GAZETTEER

GLOSSARY

INDEX

Kentucky: Political

Legend
★ State capital
• County seat
— State border
— County border

INDIANA

ILLINOIS

TENNESSEE

Ohio River

MEADE
• Brandenburg

Hawesville •
HANCOCK

Hardinsburg •

BRECKINRIDGE

HARDIN

Elizabethtown •

Henderson •
HENDERSON

Owensboro •
DAVIESS

Morganfield •
UNION

WEBSTER
Dixon •

Calhoun •
MCLEAN
Hartford •
OHIO

GRAYSON
Leitchfield •

Green River

HART
Munfordville •

CRITTENDEN
Marion •

HOPKINS
Madisonville •

EDMONSON
Brownsville •

LIVINGSTON

MUHLENBERG
Greenville •

Morgantown •
BUTLER

Smithland •

CALDWELL
Eddyville •
Princeton •

BALLARD
Wickliffe •

Paducah •
MCCRACKEN

Tennessee River

BARREN
Glasgow •

Bowling Green •
WARREN

CHRISTIAN

LOGAN

LYON

Cadiz •

Benton •
MARSHALL

Bardwell •

CARLISLE

GRAVES

Hopkinsville •

TODD
Elkton •

Russellville •

SIMPSON

Scottsville •
ALLEN

Clinton •
HICKMAN

Mayfield •

Lake Barkley

TRIGG

Franklin •

FULTON Hickman •

Murray •
CALLOWAY

Lake Kentucky

Scale
0   20   40 Miles
0   20   40 Kilometers
Albers Equal-Area Projection

R2

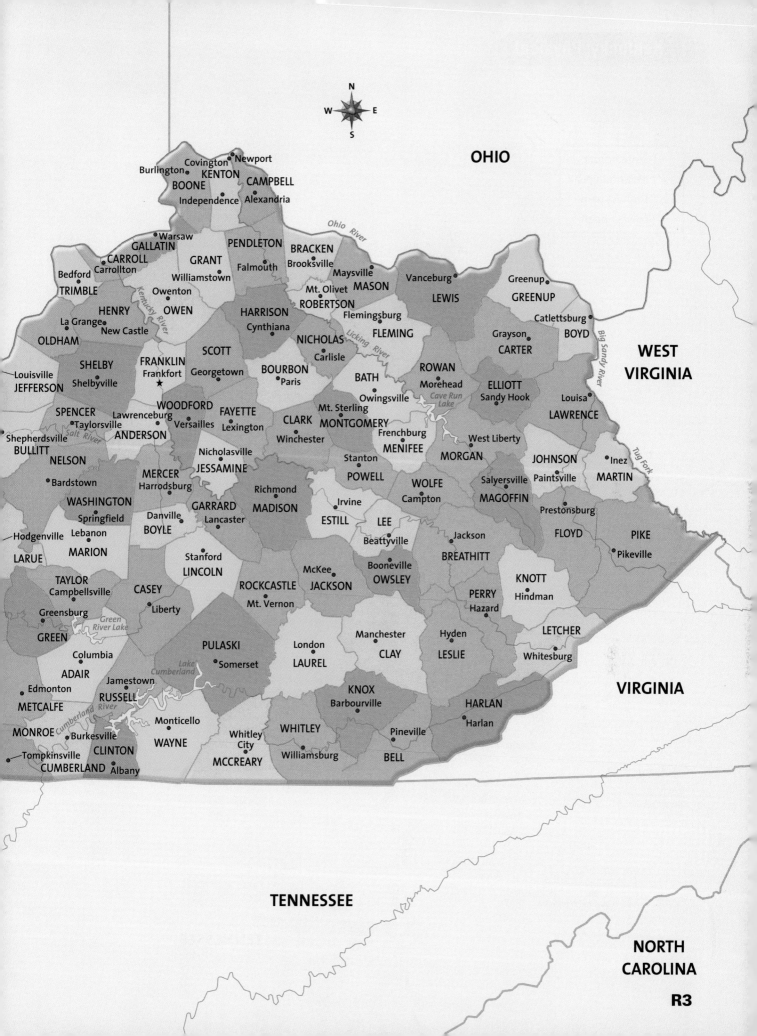

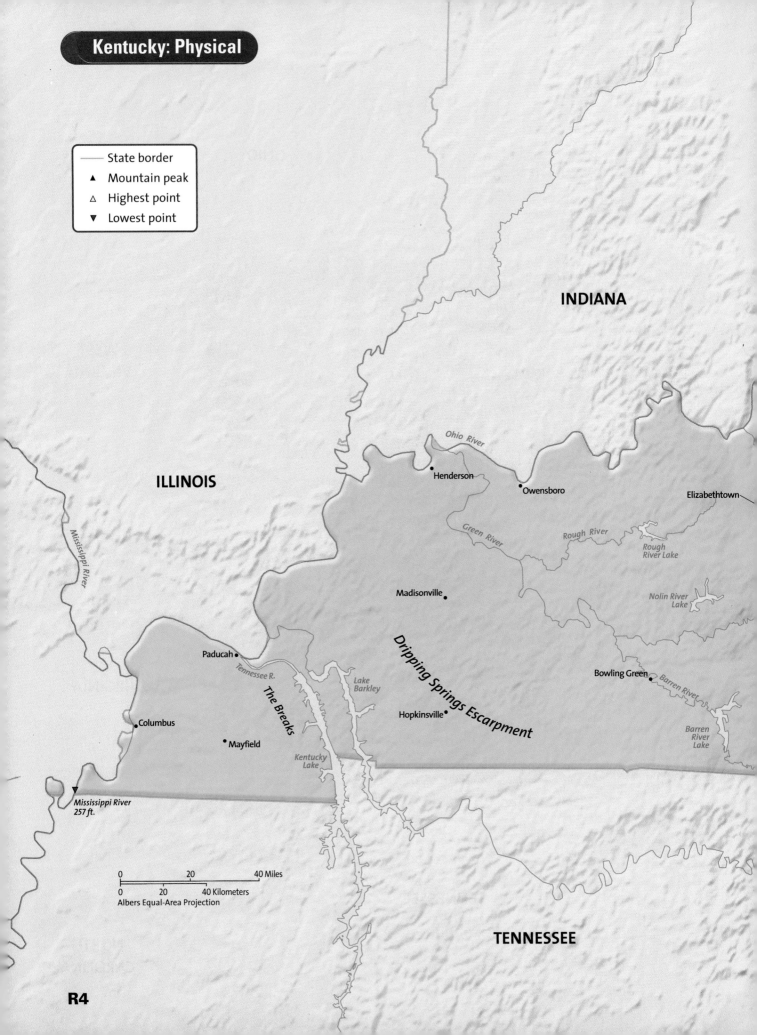

Kentucky: Physical

State border
▲ Mountain peak
△ Highest point
▼ Lowest point

INDIANA

ILLINOIS

Ohio River

Henderson

Owensboro

Elizabethtown

Green River

Rough River

Rough River Lake

Madisonville

Nolin River Lake

Paducah

Tennessee R.

Lake Barkley

Bowling Green

Barren River

The Breaks

Dripping Springs Escarpment

Hopkinsville

Columbus

Mayfield

Kentucky Lake

Barren River Lake

Mississippi River 257 ft.

0   20   40 Miles
0   20   40 Kilometers
Albers Equal-Area Projection

TENNESSEE

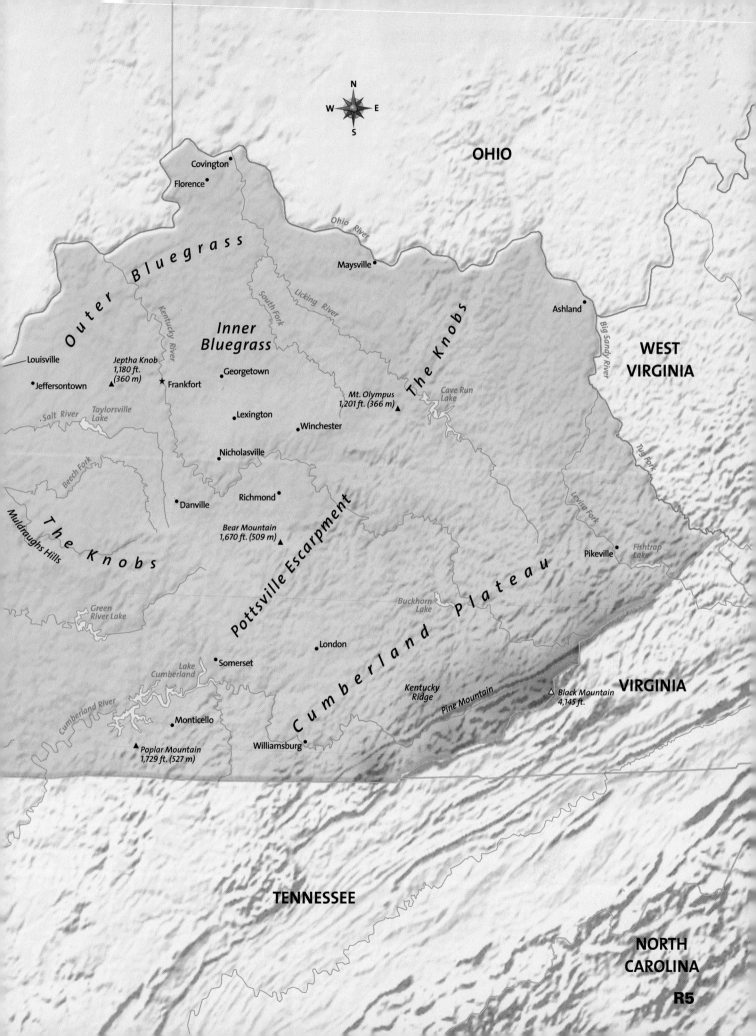

OHIO

Ohio River

Covington

Florence

Maysville

O u t e r   B l u e g r a s s

Licking River

South Fork

Ashland

Inner Bluegrass

Kentucky River

T h e   K n o b s

WEST VIRGINIA

Big Sandy River

Louisville

Jeptha Knob
1,180 ft.
(360 m)

Georgetown

Jeffersontown

★ Frankfort

Mt. Olympus
1,201 ft. (366 m)

Cave Run
Lake

Salt River

Taylorsville Lake

Lexington

Winchester

Tug Fork

Nicholasville

Beech Fork

Richmond

Danville

Levisa Fork

T h e   K n o b s

Bear Mountain
1,670 ft. (509 m)

P o t t s v i l l e   E s c a r p m e n t

Pikeville

*Fishtrap
Lake*

Muldraughs Hills

Green River Lake

Buckhorn
Lake

C u m b e r l a n d   P l a t e a u

London

Somerset

Lake Cumberland

Kentucky
Ridge

Pine Mountain

△ Black Mountain
4,145 ft.

VIRGINIA

Cumberland River

Monticello

▲ Poplar Mountain
1,729 ft. (527 m)

Williamsburg

TENNESSEE

NORTH CAROLINA

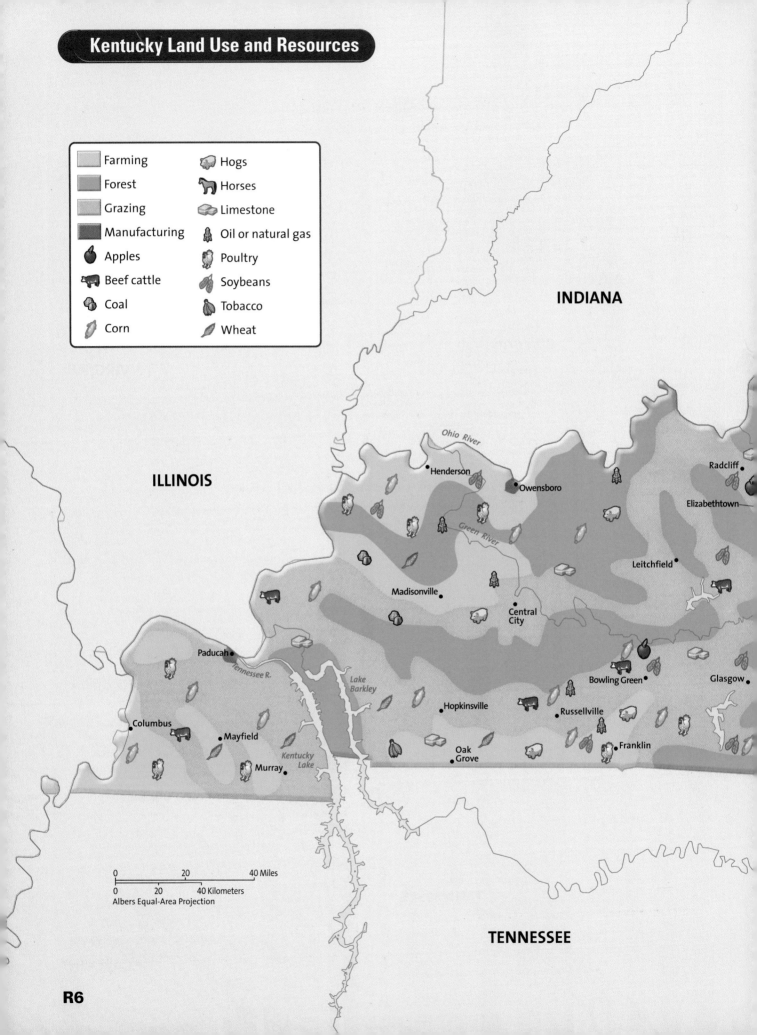

Kentucky Land Use and Resources

Legend:
- Farming
- Forest
- Grazing
- Manufacturing
- Apples
- Beef cattle
- Coal
- Corn
- Hogs
- Horses
- Limestone
- Oil or natural gas
- Poultry
- Soybeans
- Tobacco
- Wheat

INDIANA

ILLINOIS

Radcliff

Henderson

Owensboro

Elizabethtown

Ohio River

Green River

Leitchfield

Madisonville

Central City

Paducah

Tennessee R.

Lake Barkley

Bowling Green

Glasgow

Hopkinsville

Russellville

Columbus

Mayfield

Kentucky Lake

Oak Grove

Franklin

Murray

0   20   40 Miles

0   20   40 Kilometers

Albers Equal-Area Projection

TENNESSEE

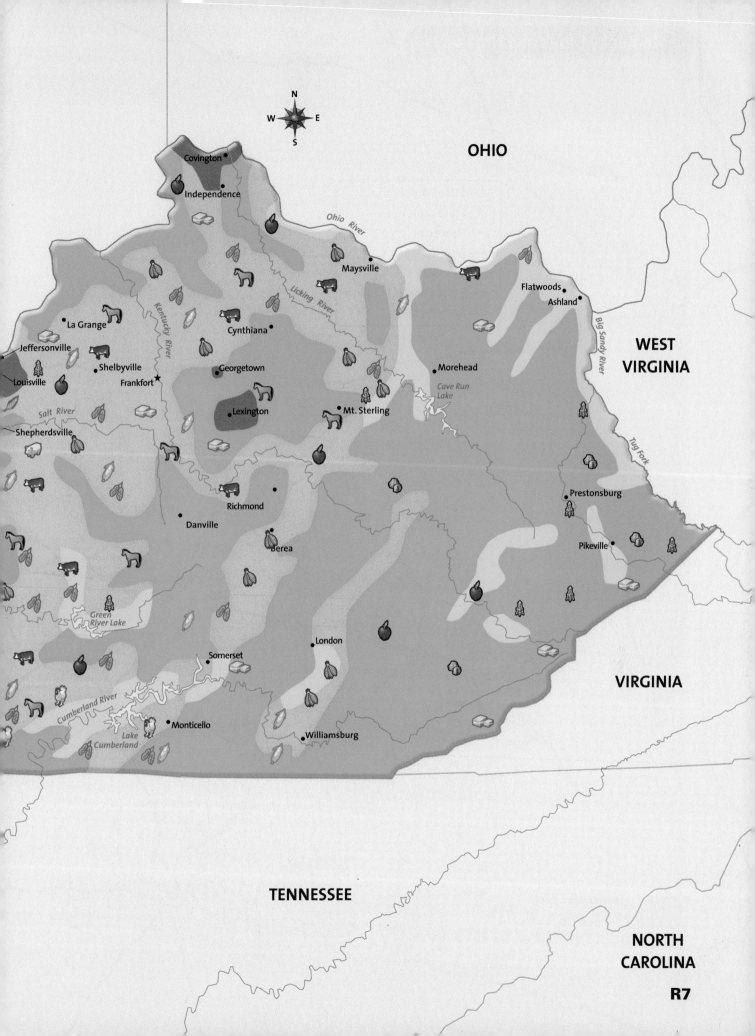

OHIO

Covington •
• Independence

Ohio River

• Maysville

Licking River

Flatwoods •
Ashland •

WEST
VIRGINIA

Big Sandy River

• La Grange

Cynthiana •

Jeffersonville •

Shelbyville •

Kentucky River

Georgetown •

• Morehead

Cave Run
Lake

Louisville

★ Frankfort

Salt River

• Lexington

• Mt. Sterling

Tug Fork

Shepherdsville •

Prestonsburg •

• Richmond

• Danville

• Berea

Pikeville •

Green
River Lake

• London

VIRGINIA

Somerset •

Cumberland River

• Monticello

Lake
Cumberland

• Williamsburg

TENNESSEE

NORTH
CAROLINA

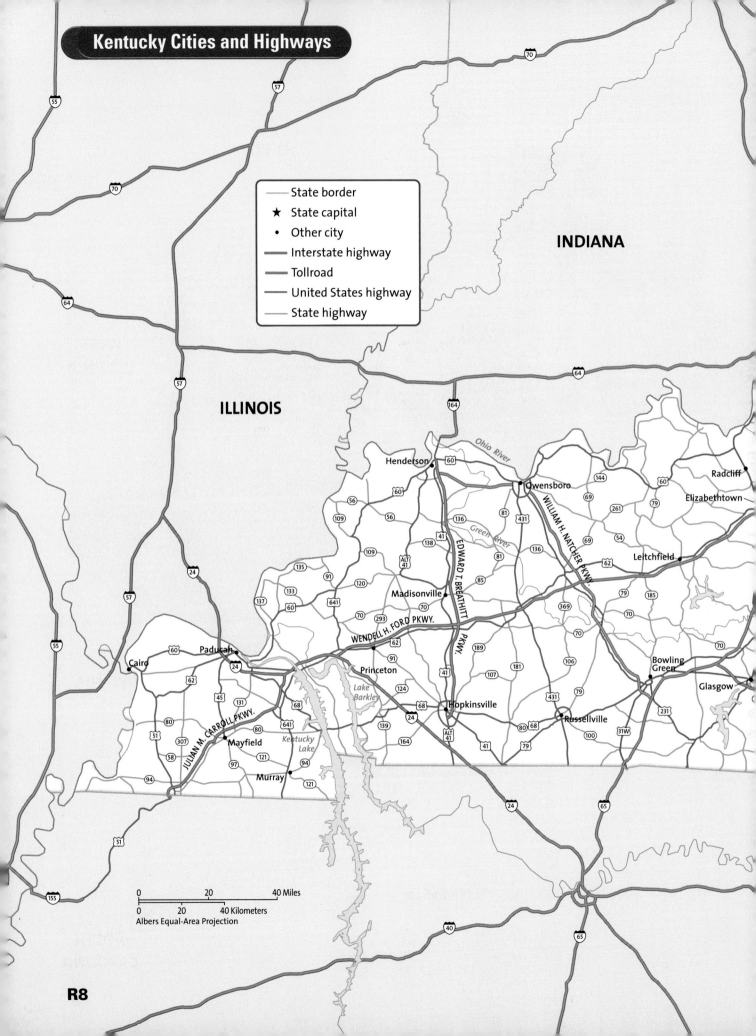

Kentucky Cities and Highways

Legend
- State border
- ★ State capital
- • Other city
- Interstate highway
- Tollroad
- United States highway
- State highway

INDIANA

ILLINOIS

Ohio River

Henderson
Owensboro
Radcliff
Elizabethtown
Leitchfield
Madisonville
Bowling Green
Glasgow
Princeton
Hopkinsville
Russellville
Cairo
Paducah
Mayfield
Murray

WILLIAM H. NATCHER PKWY.
EDWARD T. BREATHITT PKWY.
WENDELL H. FORD PKWY.
JULIAN M. CARROLL PKWY.

Green River
Lake Barkley
Kentucky Lake

0   20   40 Miles
0   20   40 Kilometers
Albers Equal-Area Projection

R8

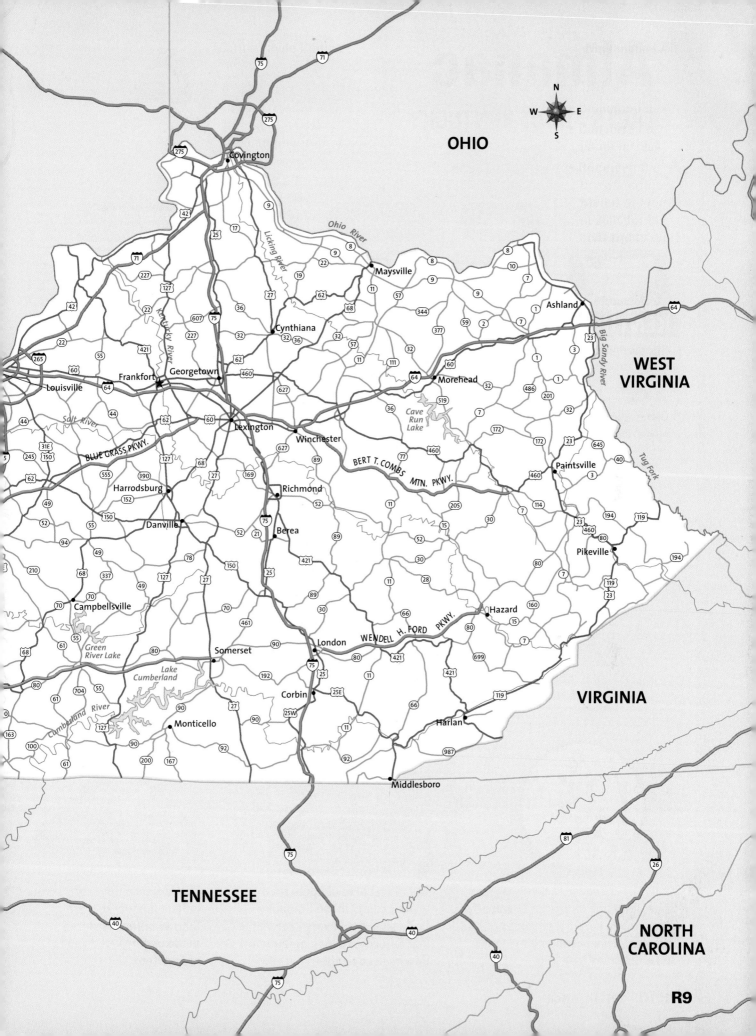

Almanac

FACTS ABOUT KENTUCKY

LAND	SIZE	CLIMATE	POPULATION*	LEADING PRODUCTS AND RESOURCES

KENTUCKY

Highest Point:
Black Mountain,
Harlan County,
4,145 feet

Lowest Point:
Mississippi River,
257 feet

Area:
40,411
square miles

Land Area:
39,732
square miles

Water Area:
679 square miles

Greatest Distance North/South:
140 miles

Greatest Distance East/West:
380 miles

Average Temperature:
Monthly average temperatures range from a high of 87.6° F to a low of 23.1° F.

Average Yearly Rainfall:
About 50 inches per year in southern Kentucky and 40 inches per year in northern Kentucky

Total Population:
4,173,405*

Population Density:
About 104 people per square mile

Crops:
Tobacco, corn, wheat, soybeans, peanuts

Livestock:
Horses, cattle, hogs

Manufacturing:
Transportation equipment, automobile and truck manufacturing, chemical manufacturing, food processing

Mining:
Anthracite coal

*the most recent figure available

Kentucky is known as the Bluegrass State. Although bluegrass is actually green, in the spring it develops purple buds that, when seen in large fields, make the grass look blue.

The oldest annual horse race in the country is the Kentucky Derby. It is held every year on the first Saturday in May at Churchill Downs in Louisville.

The largest amount of gold in the world, more than $6 billion, is stored in the underground vaults of Fort Knox.

ALMANAC

This large wooden sculpture in Paducah, Kentucky, honors the Chickasaw people who once lived in the area. It was hand carved from a local red oak tree that weighed about 56,000 pounds.

GOVERNMENT

STATE SYMBOLS

Elected Officials:
4-year terms: Governor, Lieutenant Governor, Secretary of State, Attorney General, State Auditor of Public Accounts, State Treasurer, Commissioner of Agriculture, Labor and Statistics

State Senate:
38 senators, 4-year terms

State Assembly:
100 members, 2-year terms

Counties: 120

United States Senators:
2 senators, 6-year terms

United States Representatives:
6 representatives, 2-year terms

Bird: Cardinal

Butterfly: Viceroy butterfly

Fish: Kentucky spotted bass

Flower: Goldenrod

Fruit: Blackberry

Gemstone: Freshwater pearl

Domesticated Animal: Thoroughbred horse

Wild Animal: Gray squirrel

Mineral: Coal

Musical Instrument: Appalachian dulcimer

Rock: Kentucky agate

Soil: Crider soil series

Song: "My Old Kentucky Home"

Tree: Tulip poplar

The world's longest cave is Kentucky's Mammoth Cave. The cave ranks as the second-oldest tourist attraction in the United States after Niagara Falls.

Almanac
Facts About Kentucky Counties

County	Population	County Seat
Adair	17,575	Columbia
Allen	18,541	Scottsville
Anderson	20,099	Lawrenceburg
Ballard	8,295	Wickliffe
Barren	39,473	Glasgow
Bath	11,538	Owingsville
Bell	29,672	Pineville
Boone	101,354	Burlington
Bourbon	19,623	Paris
Boyd	49,743	Catlettsburg
Boyle	28,241	Danville
Bracken	8,707	Brooksville
Breathitt	15,937	Jackson
Breckinridge	19,168	Hardinsburg
Bullitt	66,645	Shepherdsville
Butler	13,364	Morgantown
Caldwell	12,879	Princeton
Calloway	34,789	Murray
Campbell	87,256	Alexandria, Newport
Carlisle	5,310	Bardwell
Carroll	10,344	Carrollton
Carter	27,459	Grayson
Casey	16,059	Liberty
Christian	70,649	Hopkinsville
Clark	34,377	Winchester
Clay	24,254	Manchester
Clinton	9,558	Albany
Crittenden	8,999	Marion
Cumberland	7,168	Burkesville
Daviess	92,587	Owensboro

County	Population	County Seat
Edmonson	11,921	Brownsville
Elliott	6,835	Sandy Hook
Estill	15,164	Irvine
Fayette	266,358	Lexington
Fleming	14,480	Flemingsburg
Floyd	42,379	Prestonsburg
Franklin	48,142	Frankfort
Fulton	7,357	Hickman
Gallatin	7,979	Warsaw
Garrard	16,163	Lancaster
Grant	24,317	Williamstown
Graves	37,401	Mayfield
Grayson	25,004	Leitchfield
Green	11,667	Greensburg
Greenup	37,274	Greenup
Hancock	8,459	Hawesville
Hardin	96,066	Elizabethtown
Harlan	31,927	Harlan
Harrison	18,256	Cynthiana
Hart	18,237	Munfordville
Henderson	45,426	Henderson
Henry	15,771	New Castle
Hickman	5,172	Clinton
Hopkins	46,818	Madisonville
Jackson	13,622	McKee
Jefferson	700,030	Louisville
Jessamine	42,313	Nicholasville
Johnson	23,856	Paintsville
Kenton	152,890	Covington, Independence
Knott	17,582	Hindman

County	Population	County Seat
Knox	31,912	Barbourville
Larue	13,485	Hodgenville
Laurel	55,993	London
Lawrence	16,048	Louisa
Lee	7,786	Beattyville
Leslie	12,043	Hyden
Letcher	24,677	Whitesburg
Lewis	13,820	Vanceburg
Lincoln	24,821	Stanford
Livingston	9,762	Smithland
Logan	27,048	Russellville
Lyon	8,205	Eddyville
McCracken	64,700	Paducah
McCreary	17,055	Whitley City
McLean	9,982	Calhoun
Madison	76,208	Richmond
Magoffin	13,456	Salyersville
Marion	18,728	Lebanon
Marshall	30,813	Benton
Martin	12,328	Inez
Mason	16,937	Maysville
Meade	28,300	Brandenburg
Menifee	6,766	Frenchburg
Mercer	21,493	Harrodsburg
Metcalfe	10,165	Edmonton
Monroe	11,660	Tompkinsville
Montgomery	23,629	Mount Sterling
Morgan	14,360	West Liberty
Muhlenberg	31,752	Greenville
Nelson	40,406	Bardstown

County	Population	County Seat
Nicholas	7,076	Carlisle
Ohio	23,565	Hartford
Oldham	52,100	La Grange
Owen	11,300	Owenton
Owsley	4,749	Booneville
Pendleton	15,134	Falmouth
Perry	29,762	Hazard
Pike	67,080	Pikeville
Powell	13,615	Stanton
Pulaski	58,727	Somerset
Robertson	2,308	Mount Olivet
Rockcastle	16,782	Mount Vernon
Rowan	22,176	Morehead
Russell	16,838	Jamestown
Scott	38,029	Georgetown
Shelby	37,219	Shelbyville
Simpson	16,891	Franklin
Spencer	14,822	Taylorsville
Taylor	23,479	Campbellsville
Todd	11,863	Elkton
Trigg	13,249	Cadiz
Trimble	9,047	Bedford
Union	15,708	Morganfield
Warren	97,168	Bowling Green
Washington	11,266	Springfield
Wayne	20,400	Monticello
Webster	14,130	Dixon
Whitley	37,566	Williamsburg
Wolfe	7, 045	Campton
Woodford	23,961	Versailles

Almanac
Facts About Kentucky Governors

Governor	Term	Governor	Term
Isaac Shelby	1792–1796	William Owsley	1844–1848
James Garrard	1796–1804	John J. Crittenden	1848–1850
Christopher Greenup	1804–1808	John L. Helm	1850–1851
Charles Scott	1808–1812	Lazarus W. Powell	1851–1855
Isaac Shelby	1812–1816	Charles S. Morehead	1855–1859
George Madison	1816–1819	Beriah Magoffin	1859–1862
Gabriel Slaughter	1819–1820	James F. Robinson	1862–1863
John Adair	1820–1824	Thomas E. Bramlette	1863–1867
Joseph Desha	1824–1828	John L. Helm	1867
Thomas Metcalfe	1828–1832	John W. Stevenson	1867–1871
John Breathitt	1832–1834	Preston H. Leslie	1871–1875
James T. Morehead	1834–1836	James B. McCreary	1875–1879
James Clark	1836–1839	Luke P. Blackburn	1879–1883
Charles A. Wickliffe	1839–1840	James Proctor Knott	1883–1887
Robert P. Letcher	1840–1844	Simon B. Buckner	1887–1891

Governor	Term
John Young Brown	1891–1895
William O. Bradley	1895–1899
William S. Taylor	1899–1900
William J. Goebel	1900
J. C. Wickliffe Beckham	1900–1907
Augustus E. Willson	1907–1911
James B. McCreary	1911–1915
Augustus O. Stanley	1915–1919
James D. Black	1919
Edwin P. Morrow	1919–1923
William J. Fields	1923–1927
Flem D. Sampson	1927–1931
Ruby Laffoon	1931–1935
Albert B. Chandler	1935–1939
Keen Johnson	1939–1943

Governor	Term
Simeon S. Willis	1943–1947
Earle C. Clements	1947–1950
Lawrence W. Wetherby	1950–1955
Albert B. Chandler	1955–1959
Bert T. Combs	1959–1963
Edward T. Breathitt	1963–1967
Louie B. Nunn	1967–1971
Wendell H. Ford	1971–1974
Julian M. Carroll	1974–1979
John Y. Brown, Jr.	1979–1983
Martha L. Collins	1983–1987
Wallace G. Wilkinson	1987–1991
Brereton C. Jones	1991–1995
Paul E. Patton	1995–2003
Ernest L. Fletcher	2003–2007

Biographical Dictionary

The Biographical Dictionary lists many of the people introduced in this book. The page number tells where the main discussion of each person starts. See the Index for other page references.

Ali, Muhammad *1942–* A famous boxer who also worked for civil rights; awarded the Presidential Medal of Freedom in 2005. p. 171

Arthur, Gabriel *1600s* One of the first Virginians to travel to Kentucky. p. 63

Asbury, Francis *1745–1816* English-born Methodist bishop. p. 91

Audubon, John James *1785–1851* Artist whose detailed paintings of North American birds were published in *Birds of America*, a four-volume series that is still popular today. p. 167

Boone, Daniel *1734–1820* One of the first American pioneers to cross the Appalachian Mountains. p. 72

Boone, Jemima *1762–1829* Daughter of Daniel and Rebecca Boone who arrived in Kentucky with her parents in 1775. p. 73

Breckinridge, Madeline McDowell *1872–1920* National leader of the woman's suffrage movement for the right to vote. p. 127

Brown, William Wells *1815–1884* The nation's first African American novelist. p. 166

Buckner, Simon B. *1886–1945* General who commanded the United States landing forces in Japan. He was killed on Okinawa in 1945. p. 130

Bush, George W. *1946–* Forty-third U.S. President and former governor of Texas. He is the son of the forty-first President, George H. W. Bush. p. 146

Cavelier, Réne-Robert *See* La Salle.

Clark, George Rogers *1752–1818* Pioneer and American Revolutionary War hero, who was the brother of William Clark. p. 85

Clark, Doctor Thomas D. *1903–2005* A famous historian of Kentucky, the South, and the United States; served as Kentucky's State Historian for many years. p. 170

Clark, William *1770–1838* An American explorer who helped Meriwether Lewis in an expedition through the Louisiana Purchase. p. 107

Clay, Henry *1777–1852* A representative from Kentucky, who worked for compromises on the slavery issue. He became known as the Great Compromiser. p. 107

Clay, Laura *1849–1941* Well-known suffragist who served as the first president of the Kentucky Equal Rights Association from 1888 to 1912. p. 127

Clooney, Rosemary *1928–2002* American popular singer and actress. p. 161

Collins, Martha Layne *1936–* First woman Kentucky governor, who served from 1983 to 1987. p. 145

Coomes, Jane *1750–1816* A Kentucky schoolteacher who, in 1776, opened Kentucky's first school in Harrodsburg. p. 75

Cornstalk *about 1727–1777* Chief of the Shawnee who, after battling in Lord Dunmore's War, felt responsible for the loss of both Native Americans' and colonists' lives; encouraged and promoted peace with the European settlers. p. 48

Crowe, J. D. *1937–* American banjo player and bluegrass musician. p. 134

Deganawida *1500s* Iroquois leader who called for an end to the fighting among the Iroquois and helped unite the Iroquois tribes. p. 45

E

Estill, James A militia captain who, in 1782, led Kentucky settlers against a group of Wyandot and was killed in the fight. p. 86

Estill, Monk *about 1760–1835* The enslaved African servant of Captain James Estill, who fought against Native Americans and helped injured settlers. p. 86

Faulkner, Henry Lawrence *1924–1981* Artist who painted Kentucky landscapes, animals, religious figures, and other figures. p. 167

Finley, John Fur trader who helped Daniel Boone find the way across the Appalachian Mountains to Kentucky. p. 72

Ford, Henry *1863–1947* American automobile manufacturer who mass-produced cars at low cost by using assembly lines. p. 128

George III *1738–1820* British king who issued the Proclamation of 1763, giving the land west of the Appalachian Mountains to Native Americans. p. 67

Gist, Christopher *1706–1759* Explorer of the West who explored and surveyed Ohio and part of Kentucky for the Ohio Land Company in 1750. p. 63

Grant, Ulysses S. *1822–1885* Eighteenth U.S. President and, earlier, commander of the Union army in the Civil War. p. 115

Hamilton, Henry British captain who fought the American militia during the American Revolution. p. 85

Harrod, James *1742–1793* Pioneer and founder of Harrodsburg, in 1774, the first permanent settlement west of the Allegheny Mountains. p. 74

Henderson, Richard *1734–1785* Judge who hired Daniel Boone to start the settlement in Kentucky that became known as Boonesborough. p. 72

Howard, John *1726–1790* British explorer arrested by the French in 1742 for exploring land that the French believed belonged to them. p. 65

Jacob, Murv *1944–* Descendant of Kentucky Cherokee, who became an illustrator of children's books that are based upon Cherokee legends and folklore. p. 47

Jefferson, Thomas *1743–1826* Third President of the United States and the main writer of the Declaration of Independence; he sent Lewis and Clark on their expedition to explore the Louisiana Purchase. p. 107

Johnson, Lyndon B. *1908–1973* Thirty-seventh President of the United States, he awarded the Presidential Medal of Freedom to civil rights activist Whitney M. Young, Jr. p. 137

Kenton, Simon *1755–1836* Frontier explorer, soldier, and scout for Daniel Boone and George Rogers Clark. p. 84

Kimmel, Husband *1882–1968* A Kentucky admiral who commanded the fleet at Pearl Harbor at the time of the Japanese attack in 1941. p. 130

King, Martin Luther, Jr. *1929–1968* African American civil rights leader who worked for justice and fairness and the protection of individual rights in nonviolent ways, he won the Nobel Peace Prize in 1964. p. 136

Kingsolver, Barbara *1955–* Kentucky writer of novels and poems who has received many awards for her work. p. 166

Knox, Henry *1750–1806* General in the Continental Army during the American Revolution and the first United States secretary of war. p. 126

La Salle, René-Robert Cavelier, Sieur de *1643–1687* French explorer who found the mouth of the Mississippi River and claimed Kentucky and all of the Mississippi River valley for France. p. 62

Lee, Robert E. *1807–1870* General and leader of the Confederate army who surrendered to Union General Ulysses S. Grant, ending the Civil War. p. 115

Lee, Willis A. *1888–1945* Kentucky admiral who commanded United States battleships in the Pacific Ocean during World War II. p. 130

Lewis, Meriwether *1774–1809* Explorer who, with William Clark, explored the Louisiana Territory and lands west of the Rocky Mountains. p. 107

Lincoln, Abraham *1809–1865* Sixteenth President of the United States and leader of the Union in the Civil War. p. 113

Logan, Benjamin *c.1742–1802* Soldier, pioneer, and politician who was born in Virginia and settled in Kentucky. p. 93

Lynn, Loretta *1935–* Well-known country singer who wrote an autobiography called *Coal Miner's Daughter* in 1976. p. 167

Mason, Bobbie Anne *1940–* Kentucky-born writer whose novels and short stories often take place in western Kentucky. p. 166

McCormick, Cyrus *1809–1884* Inventor who built a reaping machine for harvesting wheat. p. 109

McGinty, Ann *about 1750–1815* Pioneer who settled in Harrodsburg soon after settlement in 1775. She brought the first spinning wheel to Kentucky and became Kentucky's first clothing manufacturer. p. 75

Monroe, Bill *1911–1996* Known as "The Father of Bluegrass Music," Bill Monroe made Bluegrass music famous all over the word. p. 134

Murray, John *1732–1809* Earl of Dunmore and British colonial governor of Virginia, who led the Virginians in a campaign known as Lord Dunmore's War against Native Americans. p. 71

Nicholas, George *1743–1799* Lawyer, soldier, and a drafter of the Kentucky constitution. p. 93

Paris, Malinda Robinson *1824–1892* Daughter of an enslaved man and a free woman who traveled on the Underground Railroad to freedom. p. 120

Sawyer, Diane *1945–* Well-known television journalist, who was born in Glasgow, Kentucky. p. 166

Sequoyah *about 1760–1843* Cherokee leader who created the Cherokee writing system and traveled across the United States, teaching the system to the Cherokee people. p. 49

Shelby, Isaac *1750–1826* Pioneer, soldier, and politician who became the first governor of Kentucky from 1792 to 1796. p. 95

Skaggs, Ricky *1954–* American bluegrass and country musician, singer, and composer. p. 134

Tecumseh *1768–1813* Shawnee leader in the Northwest Territory who wanted to stop British colonists from settling on Native American lands. p. 49

Trimble, Robert *1777–1828* Lawyer and United States Supreme Court Justice from 1826 to 1828. p. 187

Walker, Thomas *1715–1794* Member of the Loyal Land Company who led an expedition to explore and survey the 800,000 acres (in what is now Virginia and southeastern Kentucky) that were granted to the Loyal Land Company. p. 63

Warren, Robert Penn *1905–1989* Author and educator who won many awards for his writings and was the first Poet Laureate of the United States. p. 166

Young, Whitney M., Jr. *1921–1971* African American educator and civil rights leader who was director of the National Urban League from 1961 to 1971. p. 136

Gazetteer

The Gazetteer is a geographical dictionary that will help you locate places discussed in this book. Place names are listed alphabetically. A description tells you about each place, and the page number tells where each place appears on a map in the book. The absolute location, or latitude and longitude, of each city appears in parentheses within the description.

Appalachian Mountains (a•puh•LAY•chuhn) A mountain system of eastern North America; extends from southeastern Quebec, Canada, to central Alabama. p. 58

Atlantic Ocean Second-largest ocean; separates North and South America from Europe and Africa. p. 8

Black Mountain A peak in the Appalachian Mountains; at 4,145 feet tall, it is the highest point in Kentucky. p. 15

Bluegrass Region One of Kentucky's six natural regions; it stretches across the central part of northern Kentucky and is divided into two parts—the Inner Blugrass and the Outer Bluegrass. p. 7

Boonesborough Early Kentucky settlement started by Daniel Boone; the site is now Fort Boonesborough State Park. (38°N, 84°W) p. 59

Bowling Green A city in Kentucky, located on the Barren River; one of Kentucky's cities that has a commission-manager government. (37°N, 87°W) p. 15

Carlisle A city located in Nicholas County, in north-central Kentucky. (38°N, 84°W) p. R3

Covington A community in northern Kentucky; known for its Suspension Bridge over the Ohio River; part of the "Golden Triangle" of manufacturing cities. (39°N, 85°W) p. 15

Cumberland Falls State Park A popular natural park located southwest of Corbin, Kentucky; known for its 60-foot-tall wall of water. p. 157

Cumberland River A river in southern Kentucky and northern Tennessee that flows into the Ohio River; the Cumberland Falls is found along this river. p. 7

Cumberland Gap A pass through the Appalachian Mountains in Tennessee. p. 59

Cumberland Plateau An area of high, flat land in Kentucky just west of the Appalachian Mountains. p. 7

Danville A small town in Kentucky where leaders met to discuss problems with Virginia in 1784. (38°N, 85°W) p. 59

Eastern Kentucky Coal Field Region One of Kentucky's six natural regions; it stretches along Kentucky's eastern border and has the state's highest and most rugged land. p. 7

F

Fort Boonesborough State Park One of Kentucky's most popular natural and historic parks; named after Daniel Boone. p. 78

Fort Knox A city near Louisville, Kentucky, that began as a training camp for World War I soldiers using artillery and that continues to serve this purpose today; where the United States government stores its gold. p. 157

Frankfort The first and current capital of Kentucky; the only Union state capital to be captured during the Civil War. (38°N, 85°W) p. 15

G

Glasgow A city located in southern Kentucky; known for the Scottish Highland Games, featuring Scottish music, dancing, and athletic contests, that take place there. (37°N, 86°W) p. 156–157

Great Lakes A chain of five lakes, located in central North America; the largest group of freshwater lakes in the world. p. 58

Gulf of Mexico A body of water off the southeastern coast of North America; it is bordered by the United States, Cuba, and Mexico. p. 37

Harrodsburg The first permanent settlement in Kentucky; settlers there made the first plow that was used in the region; Ann McGinty brought there the first spinning wheel ever used in Kentucky; the place of Kentucky's first school. (38°N, 85°W) p. 72

Henry County One of Kentucky's counties; includes cities such as New Castle. p. 188

Jefferson County One of Kentucky's most densely populated counties; includes Louisville, one of Kentucky's largest cities. p. 188

Johnson County A county in eastern Kentucky; country singer Loretta Lynn grew up here. p. 188

Kaskaskia A village in southwestern Illinois; site of a major Revolutionary War battle in 1778 in which Kentuckians attacked and captured this British fort. (38°N, 90°W) p. 63

Kentucky River A river in north-central Kentucky that flows northwest into the Ohio River. Kentucky's early settlements of Harrodsburg and Boonesborough and the state capital Frankfort were founded along the Kentucky River. p. 7

The Knobs Region One of Kentucky's six natural regions; it runs along the western, southern, and eastern edges of the Bluegrass Region. p. 7

Lexington A city in north-central Kentucky; part of the Golden Triangle of manufacturing cities; known as the "Horse Capital of the World." (38°N, 84°W) p. 15

Logan's Station One of Kentucky's fortified outposts where settlers stayed during times of attack. p. 59

Louisville The largest city in Kentucky; Union forces had military headquarters here during the Civil War. (38°N, 86°W) p. 15

Mammoth Cave A system of caves in south-central Kentucky; the longest cave system in the world. (37°N, 86°W) p. 30

Mayfield A city located in Graves County in western Kentucky; birthplace of writer Bobbie Ann Mason. (38°N, 89°W) p. 18

Mill Springs The site of the 1862 Civil War battle in which Union troops held back the Confederates, preventing them from pushing farther into Kentucky. (37°N, 85°W) p. 105

Mississippi Embayment Region One of Kentucky's six natural regions; also known as the Jackson Purchase, it covers the western corner of Kentucky. p. 6

Mississippi River A river that flows from Minnesota to the Gulf of Mexico; the longest river in the United States. p. 6

Mississippian Plateau Region One of Kentucky's six natural regions; also known as the Pennyroyal Region, it covers much of west-central Kentucky. p. 7

Morgan County A county in eastern Kentucky; named for Revolutionary War General Daniel Morgan. (39°N, 83°W) p. 188

New York City The largest city in the United States; a target of terrorist attacks on September 11, 2001. (41°N, 74°W) p. 58

North America One of the world's seven continents; located in the Northern Hemisphere. p. 8

Northwest Territory A former territory of the United States, made up of the lands west of Pennsylvania, north of the Ohio River, east of the Mississippi River, and south of the Great Lakes; later became the six Great Lakes states. p. 84

O

Ohio River A tributary of the Mississippi River; begins in Pittsburgh, Pennsylvania, and ends in Cairo, Illinois. p. 6

Owensboro A city located in western Kentucky; the home of the International Bluegrass Music Association. (38°N, 87°W) p. 15

P

Perryville A city in central Kentucky and the site of a Civil War battle in 1862. (38°N, 85°W) p. 105

Pike County One of Kentucky's least densely populated counties; located in the Eastern Coal Field Region of the state. p. 188

R

Richmond A city in east-central Kentucky; Confederates captured it during the Civil War. (38°N, 84°W) p. 105

S

Shelby County A county in northern Kentucky; named for Isaac Shelby, the state's first governor. p. 188

Simpson County A county in southern Kentucky; includes cities such as Franklin; artist Henry Lawrence Faulkner lived there in the 1900s. p. 188

Southeast A region of the United States that is made up of 13 states. Kentucky is in the Southeast region. p. 10

T

Tennessee River A tributary of the Ohio River. p. 6

Trimble County A county in northern Kentucky; named after Robert Trimble, a Kentucky lawyer who became a United States Supreme Court justice. p. 188

U

United States of America A country in the Northern and Western Hemispheres that includes 49 states in North America and the state of Hawaii in the Pacific Ocean. p. 9

V

Vincennes A town in southwestern Indiana; part of the Northwest Territory; site of a Revolutionary War battle in 1779 in which Kentuckians attacked and captured the British fort. (39°N, 88°W) p. 84

Virginia One of the early English colonies in North America; now a state in the United States. p. 113

W

West Liberty A city in Morgan County in Kentucky; located on the Licking River. (38°N, 83°W) p. R3

Western Kentucky Coal Field Region One of Kentucky's six natural regions; located along the southern bank of the Ohio River; the Mississippian Plateau Region surrounds it on three sides. p. 6

Wickliffe Mounds Pyramid-shaped mounds with flat tops located in Kentucky. p. 37

GAZETTEER

Glossary

The Glossary contains important history and social science words and their definitions, listed in alphabetical order. Each word is respelled as it would be in a dictionary. When you see the mark ' after a syllable, pronounce that syllable with more force. The page number at the end of the definition tells where the word is first used in this book. Guide words at the top of each page help you quickly locate the word you need to find.

add, āce, câre, pälm; end, ēqual; it, īce; odd, ōpen, ôrder; tŏŏk, pōōl; up, bûrn; yōō as *u* in *fuse*; oil; pout; ə as *a* in *above*, e in *sicken*, i in *possible*, o in *melon*, u in *circus*; check; ring; thin; this; zh as in *vision*

A

abolitionist (a•bə•li´shən•ist) A person who wanted slavery to be outlawed. p. 113

absolute location (ab´sə•loot lō•kā´shən) The exact location of a place on Earth, either a postal location or its lines of latitude and longitude. p. 14

ally (a´lī) A partner in war. p. 66

amendment (ə•mend´mənt) An addition or change made to a constitution. p. 181

agriculture (a´grə•kul•chər) Farming. p. 35

ancestor (an´ses•tər) An early family member. p. 33

artifact (är´tə•fakt) An object made by people in the past. p. 46

B

barter (bär´tər) To trade goods, usually without using money. p. 34

bond (bänd) A loan to the United States government that the government promised to pay back. p. 125

border state (bôr´dər stāt) During the Civil War, a state that allowed slavery but did not secede from the Union. Delaware, Kentucky, Maryland, Missouri, and West Virginia were border states. p. 114

boundary (baûn´də•rē) A line or point that indicates a limit. p. 92

C

census (sen´səs) An official population count. p. 91

centennial (sen•te´nē•əl) A 100th anniversary or a celebration of this event. p. 123

ceremony (ser´ə•mō•nē) A celebration to honor a religious event or another important event. p. 37

civil rights (si´vəl rīts) The rights of citizens to equal treatment. p. 135

civil war (si´vəl wôr) A war between two groups in the same country. p. 113

civilian (sə•vil´yən) A person who is not in the military. p. 125

colonist (kä´lə•nist) A person who lives in a colony. p. 61

colony (kä´lə•nē) A land ruled by a distant country. p. 61

commercial farm (kə•mər´shəl färm) A farm that grow crops to sell. p. 173

commission (kə•mi´shən) A special committee, such as a group of people chosen to run a government. p. 189

constitution (kän•stə•tōō´shən) A plan of government. p. 93

continent (kän´tə•nənt) One of the seven largest land areas on Earth. p. 9

county (koun´tē) A section of a state. p. 187

county seat (koun´tē set) The town or city where the county government is located. p. 188

craft (kraft) A special skill used to make useful objects. p. 167

culture (kul´chər) The way of life of a group of people. p. 41

D

democracy (di•mä´krə•sē) A form of government in which people rule by making decisions for themselves, or by electing people to make decisions for them. p. 94

depression (di•pre´shən) A time of little economic growth when there are few jobs and people have little money. p. 129

E

earthwork (ûrth´wərk) A wall or mound made of dirt or stone. p. 36

economy (i•kä´nə•mē) The way in which people of a state, region, or country use resources to meet their needs. p. 133

elevation (e•lə•vā´shən) The height of land above sea level. p. 68

entrepreneur (än•trə•prə•nûr´) A person who sets up and runs a business. p. 128

equator (i•kwā´tər) An imaginary line that divides Earth into the Northern Hemisphere and the Southern Hemisphere. p. 9

erosion (i•rō´zhən) The slow wearing away of Earth's surface by wind or water. p. 19

ethnic group (eth´nik gro͞op) A group of people from the same country, or the same race, or with a shared culture. p. 160

executive branch (ig•ze´kyə•tiv branch) The branch of government that enforces, or carries out, laws. p. 182

expedition (ek•spə•di´shən) A journey of exploration. p. 107

export (ek´spôrt) A product shipped from one country to be sold in another. p. 176

extinct (ik•stingkt´) No longer in existence, which is what happens to a living thing when all of its kind have died out. p. 34

F

fertile (fûr´təl) Good for growing crops. p. 18

fort (fôrt) A strong building or area that can be defended against enemy attacks. p. 65

fossil fuel (fä´səl fyül) Animal and plant remains that over millions of years have changed to coal, oil, and gas, which are used for heat or energy. p. 26

free state (frē´ stāt) A state that did not allow slavery before the Civil War. p. 113

frontier (frən•tir´) Land that lies beyond settled areas. p. 72

G

gap (gap) An opening or a low place between mountains. p. 64

glacier (glā´shər) A huge, slow-moving field or mass of ice. p. 33

grant (grant) An official document that gives permission for something. p. 63

H

hemisphere (he´mə•sfir) A half of Earth. p. 9

high-tech (hī tek) Shortened form of the words high technology; having to do with inventing, building, or using computers and other kinds of electronic equipment. p. 145

human characteristic (hyo͞o´mən kar•ik•tə•ris´tik) Feature created by humans. p. 12

GLOSSARY

immigrant (i´mi•grənt) A person who comes from another place to live in a country. p. 160

import (im´pôrt) A good, or product, that is brought into one country from another to be sold. p. 176

independence (in•də•pen´dəns) Freedom to govern on one's own. p. 83

industry (in´dus•trē) All the businesses that make one kind of product or provide one kind of service. p. 110

interest (in´trəst) An amount that is paid for the use of money. p. 175

judicial branch (jōō•di´shəl branch) The branch of government that makes sure that laws agree with the constitution and are carried out fairly. p. 183

jury trial (jûr´ē trī´əl) A trial in which a group of citizens decides whether a person accused of a crime should be found guilty or innocent. p. 193

legend (le´jənd) A story that is handed down over time. p. 47

legislative branch (le´jəs•lā•tiv branch) The branch of government that makes laws. p. 182

limited resource (li´mə•təd rē´sors) A resource that will run out someday. p. 29

lines of latitude (līnz əv la´tə•tood) Lines that run east and west on a map or globe. p. 14

lines of longitude (līnz əv län´jə•tood) Lines that run north and south on a map or globe. p. 14

locomotive (lō•kə´mō•tiv) A railroad engine. p. 121

longhouse (lông´hous) A long bark-covered shelter built by bending poles made from young trees. p. 45

magistrate (ma´jə•strāt) An elected helper to the county judge executive. p. 188

manufacturing (man•yə•fak´chə•ring) The making of goods from raw materials by hand or by machinery. p. 122

market economy (mär´kət i•kä´nə•mē) An economic system in which people can start and run businesses with little control by the government. p. 173

metropolitan area (me•trə•pä´lə•tən âr´ē•ə) A city together with its suburbs. p. 133

militia (mə•li´shə) A volunteer army. p. 85

mineral (min´rəl) A natural resource found in rocks. p. 26

modify (mäd´ə•fī) To change. p. 26

municipal (myōō•ni´sə•pəl) Having to do with a city. p. 189

N

natural region (na´chə•rəl rē´jən) A region made up of places that share the same kinds of physical features, such as landforms, elevation, climates, or bodies of water. p. 17

natural resource (na´chə•rəl rē´sôrs) Something found in nature, such as water, soil, or minerals, that people can use to meet their needs. p. 25

navigable (na´vi•gə•bəl) Deep and wide enough for ships to use. p. 108

neutral (nōō´trəl) Not taking a side in a disagreement. p. 114

GLOSSARY

O

opportunity cost (ä•pər•tōō´nə•tē kost) The thing that is given up to get something else. p. 178

P

permanent (pər´mə•nənt) Long-lasting. p. 35

physical characteristic (fi´zi•kəl kar•ik•tə•ris´tik) Feature created by nature. p. 11

pioneer (pī•ə•nir´) A person who first settles a new place. p. 72

plain (plān) An area of flat land. p. 18

plateau (pla•tō´) An area of high, flat land with lower land around it. p. 20

political system (pə•li´ti•kəl sis´təm) A system of government. p. 184

population (päp•yə•lā´shən) The number of people who live in a place. p. 28

population density (pä•pyə•lā´shən den•sə•tə) The number of people living in an area of a certain size, usually 1 square mile or 1 square kilometer. p. 159

population distribution (po•pyə•lā´shən dis•trə•byü´shən) The way a place's population is spread throughout the place. p. 159

precipitation (pri•si•pə•tā´shən) Water that falls to Earth as rain, sleet, hail, or snow. p. 21

prime meridian (prīm mə•rid´ē•ən) A line of longitude from which all other lines of longitude are measured in degrees east or west. p. 14

proclamation (prä•klə•mā´shən) An order from a country's leader to its citizens. p. 67

product (prä´dəkt) Something that people make or grow, usually to sell. p. 25

R

region (rē´jən) An area with at least one feature that makes it different from other areas. p. 10

register (re´jə•stər) To sign up. p. 195

relative location (re´lə•tiv lō•kā´shən) Where a place is in relation to one or more other places on Earth. p. 10

relief Differences in elevation. p. 68

responsibility (ri•spän•sə•bi´lə•tē) A duty. p. 194

revolution (rev•ə•lōō´shən) A sudden, great change, such as the overthrow of a government. p. 83

rural (rŏŏr´əl) Like or having to do with a place away from a city. p. 133

S

scarcity (sker´sə•tē) The lack of a resource, product, goods or services that people want. p. 29

secede (si•sēd´) To leave the United States. p. 113

segregation (se•gri•gā´shən) The practice of keeping people of one race or culture separate from other people. p. 135

self-sufficient (self sə•fish´ənt) Able to do everything for oneself, with no help from other people. p. 76

service industry (sər´vəs in´dəs•trē) An industry that does things for people instead of making things. p. 174

sharecropping (sher´kräp•ing) A form of payment in which landowners paid workers in shares of crops. p. 120

shortage (shor´tij) A lack of something. p. 130

sinkhole (sink´hōl) A large bowl-shaped hole that forms when limestone layers above underground holes collapse. p. 21

slave state (slāv stāt) A state that allowed slavery before the Civil War p. 113

slavery (slā´vər•ē) The practice of treating people as property. p. 113

specialization (spe•shə•lə•zā´shən) Focusing on one or more industries based on a region's resources, the needs of its people, and the needs of people in other regions. p. 176

specialize (spe´shə•līz) To work at one kind of job and learn to do it well. p. 42

stagecoach (stāj´kōch) An enclosed wagon that carried passengers and was pulled by horses. p. 108

station (stā´shən) A fortified outpost that is smaller than a fort. p. 84

steamboat (stēm´bōt) A boat powered by a steam engine that turns a large paddle wheel. p. 108

suburb (sub´ərb) A town or small city near a large city. p. 133

suffrage (su´frij) The right to vote in national and other elections. p. 127

surplus (sûr´pləs) An amount that is more than what is needed. p. 109

tax (taks) Money that a government collects to pay for the services it provides. p. 83

terrorist (ter´ər•ist) A person who uses violence to promote a cause. p. 146

textile (tek´stīl) Cloth. p. 110

tourism (toor´iz•əm) The business of serving visitors. p. 174

trade-off (trād´ ôf) Giving up one thing to get something else. p. 178

tribe (trīb) A group of people who share the same language, land, and leaders. p. 41

unemployment (ən•im•plôi•mənt) The number of workers without jobs. 129

urban (ûr´bən) Of or like a city. p. 133

volunteer (vä•lən•tir´) A person who does something useful without being paid for it. p. 195

wigwam (wig´wäm) A round, bark-covered shelter. p. 44

Index

The Index lets you know where information about important people, places and events appear in the book. All entries are listed in alphabetical order. For each entry, the page reference indicates where information about that entry can be found in the text. Page references for illustrations are set in italic type. An italic *m* indicates a map. Page references set in boldface type indicate the pages on which vocabulary terms are defined. Guide words at the top of each page help you identify which words appear on each page.

A

Abolitionists, **113**, R22
Absolute location, **14**, R22
Adena, 36–37
Afghanistan, 146–147
African Americans
    in civil rights movement, 135
    leaders, 136–137, *137*
Agriculture, 35, 36, R22; *see also*
    Farming and farmland
Ali, Muhammad, 171, R16
Ally, **66**, 131, 146, R22
Almanac, R10–R15
Amendment, **181**, R22
American Revolution, 82–89, *83*,
    m84, 86
Ancestors, **33**, 37, 160, R22
Ancient Puebloans, *m37*
Animals
    bears, 20, *33*
    beavers, 13
    cattle, 26, 91, 119, 173
    chickens, 173
    deer, *11*, 13, 20, *34*, 44
    elk, *34*
    hogs, *26*
    horses, 18, *19*, 26, *75*, *77*, 91, 108,
        109, 110, 119, 121, 143, *168*, 173,
        177
    mammoth, *32*, 33
    mastadon, 33
    otters, 20
    rabbits, *34*
    salmon, *107*
    turkeys, 20, 44
Appalachia region, 13
Appalachian Mountains, *13*, 17, 20,
    m63, 64, 67, 93
Appomattox Court House,
    Virginia, 115
Archaic Indians, 34
Arthur, Gabriel, 63, R16
Artifact, **46**, 76, 84, R22
Artillery, 126
Artists, 18, 167
Asbury, Francis, 91, R16
Atlas, R2–R9
Audubon, John James, 18, 167, R16
Automobile, 128, *128*, 145, *174*

B

Banks, 174
Barrens, The, 21
Barter, **34**, R22
Baskets and basket weaving, 34, 167
Battle of Blue Licks, The, *86*, 86-87
Battle of Bunker Hill, The, *82*
Battle of Little Mountain, The, 86
Bible Belt, 162
Bicentennial stamp, *123*
Biographical Dictionary, R16–R18
Biographies
    Ali, Muhammad, 171
    Boone, Daniel, 88
    Breckinridge, Madeline
        McDowell, 141
    Clark, Doctor Thomas D., 170
    Clay, Henry, 140
    Coomes, Jane, 89
    Cornstalk, 48
    Estill, Monk, 89
    Lynn, Loretta, 171
    Sequoyah, 49
    Tecumseh, 49
    Young, Whitney M., Jr., 141
Birds of America, books, 167
Black Mountain, 20, R19
"Blue Moon of Kentucky", song, 134
Bluegrass music, 134,
Bluegrass plant, *19*
Bluegrass Region, Inner and Outer,
    18–19, *m18*, 44, 111, R19
Bluegrass State, 19
Boats and ships, 34, *90–91*, *107*,
    108–109, 124, 130, 177
Bond, **125**, *125*, R22
Boone, Daniel, *72*, 72–73, 84, 85,
    108, R16
Boone, Jemima, *73*, 73
Boonesborough, 73, 84, R19
Border state, **114**, R22
Borders, 10–11, 20, 22, 23
Boundary, **92**, R22
Bowling Green, 189, R19
Branches of government
    in Kentucky, 94–95, 182–183, *183*
    in the United States, 182–183, *183*
Breckinridge, Madeline, 127, R16
Britain
    explorers, 63–64
    forts, *65*
    settlers, 61, 71
    See also American Revolution;
        French and Indian War

Brown, William Wells, 166, R16
Buckner, General Simon B., 130, R16
Bush, President George W., 146, R16

C

Canada, *m8*, 10, 120
Canoes, 44, *62*, 74
Capital, state, 12, 19, 94, 182
Capitol, state, *181*
Caring, 49, 89, 171
Census, **91**, R22
Centennial, **123**, *123*, R22
Ceremony, **37**, R22
Chart and Graph Skills
    Read a Double-Bar Graph, 138–139,
        139
Cherokee, *41*, 42, 47, 49
Chickasaw, *40*, 43, *43*, 107
Children in History
    Cherokee Children, 42
    Jemima Boone, 73
    Malinda Robinson Paris, 120
Churches, 162
Cities, 19, 133
Citizenship, 192–197, *193*
Civic leaders, 140–141
Civil rights, 127, **135**, 136–137, 141,
    R22
Civil War, 113, 112–115, *m114*, R22
Civilian, **125**, R22
Clark, Doctor Thomas D., 154,
    170, R16
Clark, George Rogers, 85, *85*, R16
Clark, William, 107, R16
Clay, Cassius Marcellus, 127
Clay, Henry, 107, 127, R16
Clay, Laura, 127, *127*, R16
Climate, 11, 17, 33–34
Clooney, Rosemary, 161, R16
Coal, 12, 20, 22, 25, 26, 27, 29, 122,
    122–123, 125, 133; *see also* Mining
"Coal Miner's Daughter, The", song,
    167
Colleges and universities, 165, *165*;
    See also Schools
Collins, Martha Layne, *145*, R16
Colonist, **61**, R22
Colony, **61**, R22
Commercial farms, 173, R22
Commission, **189**, R22
Commonwealth of Kentucky, 181

INDEX

INDEX